AUSTRALIAN RETROSPECTIVES

RELIGION IN AUSTRALIA

A History

ROGER C. THOMPSON

Series Editor
DAVID WALKER

Melbourne
OXFORD UNIVERSITY PRESS
Oxford Auckland New York

OXFORD UNIVERSITY PRESS

Oxford New York
Athens Auckland Bangkok Bombay
Calcutta Cape Town Dar es Salaam Delhi
Florence Hong Kong Istanbul Karachi
Kuala Lumpur Madras Madrid Melbourne
Mexico City Nairobi Paris Singapore
Taipei Tokyo Toronto
and associated companies in
Berlin Ibadan

OXFORD is a trade mark of Oxford University Press

First published 1994

National Library of Australia
Cataloguing-in-Publication data:

Thompson, Roger C. (Roger Clark), 1941–.
Religion in Australia: a history

Bibliography
Includes index
ISBN 0 19 5535162

1. Church and state - Australia - History. 2. Religion and politics - Australia - History.
3. Christianity - Australia - History. 4. Australia - Church history. I. Title. (Series: Australian retrospectives).

280.0994

Cover: Margaret Preston, Australia 1875–1963 'Christ turning the water into wine', 1951. Colour stencil on black paper 43.0 x 43.0 cm. Bequest W.G.Preston, the artist's widower 1977. Art Gallery NSW.
Cover designed by Jo Waite

Typeset and printed by SRM Production Services, Malaysia.
Published by Oxford University Press,
253 Normanby Road, South Melbourne, Australia.

Series Foreword

In this series we have invited authors to examine formative issues in our national history in a style accessible to non-specialists. A number of authors have responded enthusiastically to this project, welcoming the opportunity it provides to address major questions in a brisk and intelligently speculative manner. No book in this series is designed to be the last word on its subject.

By treating major themes over an extended period, *Australian Retrospectives* will bring a historical perspective to bear on matters of vital concern to Australians in the 1990s.

James Jupp's study of immigration proved an excellent starting point. Immigration has been at or near the centre of Australia's white history for almost two hundred years. The pace of Asian immigration and the environmental impacts of population increases are high on the list of immigration-related public controversies. *Implicated: The US in Australia*, the second publication in the series, is an incisive, fully researched study of the Australian–American relationship from 1788 to the present. In *The Unforgiving Minute*, the third book in the series, Graeme Davison provides the only study we have of the meaning and measurement of time in its Australian context. At a stroke, Davison has opened new territory in this fresh and imaginative study.

In the latest books in the series, Beverley Kingston brings her rich knowledge of Australian history and its source materials to bear on the subject of Shopping, a crucial factor in Australian economic history and vital to an understanding of Australian interactions with the wider world. Like its predecessors, this book presents a bold, compact and well argued case for its subject.

The impact of religion on Australian life has often been noted and the lack of studies of the subject frequently lamented. In *Religion in Australia*, Roger C. Thompson makes a persuasive case for the conservative impact of religion on Australian political life and culture. He moves deftly across space and time to bring an Australia-wide perspective to his subject.

We can be excused for calling *Australian Retrospectives* a timely publishing initiative. We have a talented pool of authors to draw from and a nation of readers demanding intellectual nourishment. We hope to honour their intelligent interest in Australia at a time when the nation is calling for new ideas and new ways of communicating them.

David Walker
Centre for Australian Studies
Deakin University

CONTENTS

ABBREVIATIONS

ABC	Australian Broadcasting Commission
ABM	Australian Board of Missions
ACC	Australian Council of Churches
ACT	Australian Capital Territory
ACTU	Australian Council of Trade Unions
ACWCC	Australian Council of the World Council of Churches
AEC	Australian Episcopal Conference
AEF	Aboriginal Evangelical Fellowship
AIM	Aborigines Inland Mission
APNR	Association for the Protection of Native Races
ASCM	Australian Student Christian Movement
AWD	Action for World Development
AWU	Australian Workers' Union
CCJP	Catholic Commission for Justice and Peace
CMS	Church Missionary Society
CSOM	Christian Social Order Movement
CSSM	Catholic Social Studies Movement (the Movement)
DAB	Dictionary of Australian Biography
DLP	Democratic Labor Party
FIA	Federated Ironworkers' Association
LCP	Liberal and Country Parties
LNP	Liberal and National Parties
MLC	Methodist Ladies College
NCC	National Civic Council
NMCA	National Missionary Council of Australia
QLP	Queensland Labor Party
TLC	Trades and Labour Council
UAM	United Aborigines Mission
UAP	United Australia Party
WCTU	Women's Christian Temperance Union

PREFACE

This is a book about the influence of religion in Australian history. Religion is defined in the broad terms used by A. C. Bouquet in his influential book, *Comparative Religion*, as 'a fixed relationship between the human self and some non-human entity, the Sacred, the Supernatural, the Self Existent, the Absolute, or simply "God"'.[1] Consequently, this book is not just about the influence of Christianity. It will consider Aboriginal spirituality, Judaism and other religions that have had an impact on Australian history.

But the main emphasis in the book is Christianity, because it has been by far the major religious influence in Australia after the arrival of the Europeans who dominate modern Australia's population. It is a subject much neglected in the past, as can be seen in the absence or scarce attention to religion in much Australian historical writing. However, in recent years there has been a boom in publishing about the history of Christianity in Australia. There is a good general history by Michael Hogan, and another good one by Ian Breward.[2] Breward's book provides a wealth of information about church life and developments not covered in this book which considers much more the impact of churches on political and other Australian life. In part, I follow a pattern established by Hogan, whose main concern was to investigate the sectarian impact of religion in Australia but provides a wider-Australia focus, whereas I draw on much newer information and consider the broader impact of religions in Australia.

The major theme of this book is the conservative influence of religion in Australian history. One way of doing this is to demonstrate the minority status of Christian radicalism. Conservatism is defined as support of the socio-economic and political status quo. Even the Catholic influence in the Australian Labor Party can be demonstrated as a conservative bulwark against socialist ideas. The term 'Protestant' is used to include the Church of England in accordance with general Australian usage. The term 'Anglican' is used to describe members of the Church of England in Australia, even though it was not called the Anglican Church in Australia until 1981. I am a practising Christian—an elder and lay preacher in the Uniting Church, and draw upon my own and others' personal experiences, as well as wide reading in relevant literature. It should be noted that this book is a synthesis of the wealth of publications in the subject rather than the product of primary source research. Hopefully, it might encourage the research needed for a more comprehensive history of the influence of religion in Australia.

In writing the book, I wish to thank Peter Dennis for recommending me to Oxford University Press. Thanks are also due to Ian Breward, who provided encouragement to write the book; to Ewan Morris, Grace Koch and Caesar D'Mello who provided valuable information; to Elizabeth Greenhalgh who proofread the text and helped compile the index; to my academic colleagues at St Mark's Institute of Theology who offered critical comments; and to the librarians of the Australian Defence Force Academy and St Mark's, who allowed me to borrow many books at the one time. Lastly, but not least, I wish to thank my wife, Sheila, who supported and endured patiently yet another rushed effort to meet a publisher's deadline.

Roger C. Thompson

CHAPTER ONE

CHRISTIANITY AND EARLY EUROPEAN SETTLEMENT, *1788–1840*

The European settlement established in Australia in 1788 had a unique purpose. It was a remote prison for criminals mainly from English cities, a condition that significantly influenced its religious character. The Christian Church was enrolled as a guardian of social order. In the official instructions to the first Lieutenant-Governor of New South Wales, naval captain Arthur Phillip, he was ordered to 'enforce a due observance of religion and good order among the inhabitants of the new settlement, and that you do take such steps for the due celebration of publick [*sic*] worship as circumstances will permit'.[1] This chapter discusses the relationships between the Christian Church and the state, convicts and the Aboriginal inhabitants from 1788 to the 1830s.

Clergy, convicts and the state

In Great Britain in the eighteenth century there were legal ties between Protestant churches and the state with the Church of England the established church of England, Wales and Ireland, and the Church of Scotland the established church of Scotland. The Church of Scotland, or Presbyterian Church, was influenced by the Calvinist branch of the sixteenth century reformation, with its emphasis on original sin, the Presbyterian form of church government by assemblies of clergy and laity, the sanctification of hard work and the importance of education. Disagreements over fine theological points also prompted breakaway movements from the Church of Scotland.

The Church of England's authority had slipped by the eighteenth century. Old laws enforcing compulsory attendance at Anglican church services had given way to an age of voluntarism. A result was that many, especially working-class people, had stopped attending. Nor had the church kept pace with new areas of population growth with the development of commerce and beginnings of industrialisation. Furthermore, there were divisions within Anglican ranks. There were high churchmen whose outlook was influenced by the Catholic origins of the church. Broad churchmen were influenced more by the eighteenth-century enlightenment, with its emphasis on order and reason, and were infected by a 'deist' outlook which emphasised creator God more than the saving grace of Jesus Christ.

There had been an evangelical revival within the Church of England called the Methodist movement or Methodism. It emphasised faith in Jesus, personal holiness, and emotional forms of worship. It also had its own organised system of lay preachers. By the 1790s, Methodism, led by the peripatetic and charismatic Anglican priest, John Wesley, was showing signs of becoming a separate denomination under the weight of strong disapproval by many bishops and clergy. However, there was also an emerging evangelical movement within the Church of England with a similar emphasis on personal faith in Jesus and his saving grace, though at this stage they were only a small minority.

Eighteenth century voluntarism also assisted the dissenting or nonconformist churches in England. These Congregationalists, English Presbyterians, Baptists, Quakers and Unitarians had been suffering persecution and discrimination. They now had freedom of worship, but were still shut out of the universities and public office. Consequently they had high representation in industry and commerce and established their own educational institutions. The history of discrimination made nonconformist denominations strong opponents of established links between church and state.

Suffering more discrimination was the Roman Catholic Church. It was the national church of many Irish people, whose attachment to it was enhanced by English overlordship. Only in Northern Ireland, where there had been an influx of Scottish Presbyterian settlers, was there any popular allegiance to another religious faith in Ireland. Superstition rather than religious understanding characterised many

Catholics, and priests held much power over parishioners. The close relationship between the Catholic Church and Irish nationalism solidified Catholic allegiance even among Irish migrants to Australia who were long denied any priests or sacramental rights.

Such religious diversity among the first European settlers to Australia posed a major threat to the perpetuation of the early alliance between church and state. Indeed, from the beginning there was a potential challenge to the role of the church as a guardian of the convict order. The appointment of the first Christian chaplain to the colony, Richard Johnson, had been influenced by the small group of Anglican evangelicals, through the agency of a member of parliament, William Wilberforce. Consequently, there were ingredients for conflict between the evangelical Johnson and broad or high church government officials. Johnson saw his main mission as converting European and native inhabitants of the colony to a personal Christianity. Potentially, this mission also conflicted with Johnson's task of assisting the maintenance of social order.

Initially, Governor Phillip had sympathy with Johnson's ministry in the colony. But his successor in December 1792, Major Francis Grose, saw little point in converting degraded convicts. He was soon damning Johnson as a Methodist — a term in conservative eyes akin to 'Jacobin' in this age of paranoia about the radicalism of the French Revolution. In fact, Johnson was a loyal subject of the British crown who regarded convicts as 'my fellow creatures'.[2] The conflict between governor and cleric ended with Grose's departure after two years. Before he left Australia at the end of 1800 Johnson found the next two governors, more sympathetic to his work. John Hunter had trained for the Presbyterian ministry and acknowledged Christ as his personal saviour. Philip King was concerned to increase the church's authority in the colony.

However, Johnson had little success with the convicts, even though he had a sympathetic interest in their welfare. He was a member of the prison establishment, acting as magistrate as well as priest. More fundamentally, most of the convicts came from the urban British working class which had become alienated from the Church of England in the eighteenth-century age of voluntarism, though many Irish convicts retained their nationalistic allegiance to the Roman Catholic Church. But the small minority of Irish convicts were given no Catholic priests because they might become a focus for sedition. In the new colony all convicts were expected to attend compulsory

Anglican worship — a further recipe for alienation from religion. This was soon demonstrated by the dwindling of Johnson's congregations to mere handfuls during Grose's era. In the period of the more sympathetic Hunter and King later increases in church attendance were caused more by efforts to promote compulsory attendance rather than by religious enthusiasm. Hunter wrote in 1798: 'a more wicked, abandon'd, and irreligious set of people have never been brought together in any part of the wo'ld'.[3]

Johnson's successor as principal chaplain, Samuel Marsden, had been appointed to assist Johnson in 1794. Initially as priest and magistrate at Parramatta, Marsden remained on good terms with the colony's governors. But this broke down after the appointment in 1810 of Lieutenant-Governor Lachlan Macquarie, a British army colonel.

At first Marsden favoured Macquarie's concern to impose a new moral order on a colony notorious for its sexual laxity. Such immorality reflected both the libertarian influences — for men — of the eighteenth-century enlightenment and the fact that most of the colony's small minority of women were convicts who were generally regarded as whores and degraded strumpets and used accordingly. Despite his own deistic Anglican faith, which had little spiritual content, Macquarie was acting in line with the evangelicals' concern for righteous living. Marsden was pleased also at Macquarie's policies of ordering compulsory church attendance for convicts in government service, and enforcing laws against the profanation of Sundays by arresting loiterers and charging publicans who traded during hours of worship.

Marsden's complaints about Macquarie stemmed from the governor's authoritarianism and his convict policy. Macquarie dictated to the church by prohibiting Marsden's move to introduce a new version of the psalms, which the governor branded as 'Methodistical', and by ordering Marsden to read government notices in services of worship. More upsetting, was Macquarie's pardoning of and reliance upon former convicts, even to the extent of appointing them as magistrates. Magistrate Marsden was horrified at being asked to associate with ex-convicts who were living with unmarried women. This offended both his sense of upholding the established social order and his concern to promote sexual morality. Thereby Marsden became a strident ally of the small group of conservative free citizens who felt that their social status and authority was being supplanted and who loudly complained of Macquarie's despotism and laxity towards convicts.

Marsden therefore contributed to the alienation of the church from the majority of the population who had some past or present personal contact with convictism. This was reinforced by Marsden's reputation as a magistrate who handed out savage flogging sentences. His role of moral policeman branded him a 'kill joy', emphasised by the judgmental tone of his evangelical preaching. Similar was the religious style of other Anglican chaplains who arrived in the colony from 1809. While none achieved such a severe reputation as Marsden, the practice of appointing Anglican clergymen as magistrates continued to 1827 and reinforced the identification between church and oppressive state.

Christians and Aborigines

The early Christian Church in Australia had even less success with Aborigines, who numbered as many as 750,000 in 1788. English Evangelicals believed the overseas heathen needed to be taught English language and customs before they could receive the Christian message. This approach was of little use among Australia's indigenous people whose culture was so well adapted to their environment and was supported by a complex system of religious beliefs that had evolved over thousands of years. Myths of the dreamtime explained the evolution of their world and the ways forest, grassland and desert environments influenced their life-styles. They worshipped spirits dwelling in sacred places in the land, which gave meaning to their lives. But Johnson and his contemporaries had no respect for Aboriginal culture or religion. To Hunter, they were a 'wretched and miserable' people and 'no signs of any religion have been observed among them'.[4]

Marsden and his Anglican contemporaries made no impression on Aborigines. Marsden failed to make an Aboriginal child, whom he fostered, into a permanently civilised European. By 1819 he had decided that 'The Aborigines are the most degraded of the human race . . . the time is not yet arrived for them to receive the great blessings of civilisation and the knowledge of Christianity'.[5] Instead, he devoted his considerable missionary energy to the Maoris of New Zealand who showed much more eagerness to appropriate for themselves the technology of European civilisation.

A major problem for the Christian church in Australia was that its clergy were imbued with a prejudice that Aboriginal lifestyles were incompatible with the Christian gospel. A partial exception was the

London Missionary Society's Lancelot Threkeld. He believed it necessary to learn an Aboriginal language and to live among Aborigines. He put this belief into practice from 1825 among the Awabakal people of the Lake Macquarie district. He also acted as an advocate for Aborigines, complaining in 1837 that 'a war of expiration [had] long existed ... with many ... atrocious acts of cruelty', to which most of his fellow Christian clergy closed their eyes.[6] But Threkeld still thought in Eurocentric terms of encouraging Aborigines to join an agricultural settlement.

Indeed, Threkeld won no apparent converts, and in 1841 his government financial support was terminated by Governor George Gipps. However, this was not because Gipps was anti-Aborigine. He was the first governor in New South Wales to attempt to tackle the problem of the destruction of Aboriginal society to the extent of arresting eleven of the perpetrators of the 1838 Myall Creek massacre and hanging the seven who were convicted of murder, despite a hysterical white community campaign to release them. This action was in line with a new evangelical influence at the British Colonial Office, which upheld Gipps on this issue. But many Australian clergy considered missions to the Aborigines a waste of effort. Marsden opposed Threkeld's mission and influenced the London Missionary Society to withdraw its support.

An attempt to meet Aborigines on their own terms occurred in the Swan River settlement in Western Australia, after the Pinjarra massacre of 1834, a barbaric repression of indigenous people who had been resisting the encroachment of settlers into their territory. Francis Armstrong, a prominent Wesleyan Methodist, who was one of the few settlers who had shown an interest in learning an Aboriginal language, established the Mt Eliza mission station. It differed from previous Australian missions by establishing a place where Aborigines could come and go as they pleased. Those who came to the settlement were paid in food for community work and assistance in building huts. But they could choose not to work and gather food in traditional ways. They were given protection from whites and other Aborigines. Mt Eliza was initially popular for people who had been cowed by the savagery of the Pinjarra massacre, an ambush which killed over twenty-five men, women and children, and which was followed by additional violent white oppression. However, in 1838 Mt Eliza closed down. Aborigines had rejected the hidden agenda of enticing them into a settled agricultural lifestyle. Not even Armstrong with his knowledge of and sympathy for Aboriginal people could appreciate the essential mobility of Aboriginal culture.

One other Christian 'solution' to the Aboriginal problem was proposed for the Tasmanian Aborigines by Governor Sir George Arthur, a fervent Anglican evangelical. His reaction to the unwillingness of indigenous Tasmanians to adopt European customs and who, especially from 1825, expressed their hostility by spearing the sheep, cattle and settlers who invaded their land, was to force them into a reserve in order to convert them to Christianity. However, only two of those Aborigines who had survived the disease and wanton murders imposed on them by Europeans, which the Christian churches in Tasmania had almost completely ignored, were captured in a dragnet sweep in 1830 by 2000 armed soldiers and settlers across the whole island. But a Wesleyan settler, George Augustus Robinson, who in 1823 had fled from financial scandal in England, had much more success, after Governor Arthur appointed him as an official conciliator for the Aborigines. Like Threkeld, he had spent time learning Aboriginal customs and an indigenous language. On extensive journeys through the island, helped by some Aborigines whose confidence he had won, Robinson gathered scores of horrific stories of how whites had mistreated indigenous Tasmanians. He thus posed as their protector. Consequently, by December 1834 he was able to persuade or capture all of the 300 or so survivors of the estimated 4500 Aborigines in Tasmania in 1788. He was richly rewarded by Governor Arthur and grateful settlers for his efforts. Only 123 Aborigines survived their journey to terminal exile on wind-swept Flinders Island in Bass Strait.

Early Anglican ascendancy

Samuel Marsden contributed to strained relations between the Protestant majority and the growing minority of Catholics. He resolutely opposed the immigration of any Roman Catholic priest to the colony, which the government had supported after the abortive rebellion by 300 Irish convicts at Castle Hill in 1804. In 1812 Marsden wrote: 'We have now cleared the Colony of all the catholic priests, have schools established in almost every district so that the rising generation will be brought up in the principles of the Protestant religion'.[7] However, this supremacy was eroded after the Napoleonic Wars, which had kept alive a strong British fear of French-influenced Irish rebellions, and because of pressure from the Catholic communities in Australia and England. In 1819 Britain appointed two chaplains for Catholics, whose numbers in New South Wales had swollen to 31% of the European population by 1828.[8]

Initially, Marsden's evangelicalism prompted him to support other Protestant bodies in the colony, such as London Missionary Society refugees from Tahitian hostility in 1798 and the Wesleyan Methodist, the Rev. Samuel Lee, who arrived without official permission in 1815. Now a separate denomination, Methodism introduced a belief in the equality of all men before God, enthusiastic hymn singing, the fervour of class meetings, and the extra-clerical manpower of lay preachers. These were ingredients for denominational growth. But the rapidly increasing number of Methodists in New South Wales soured Marsden's disposition towards them. By the 1820s he complained about Methodist poaching of Anglican Sunday school children and about Methodists' freedom to conduct worship services in competition with established Anglican parishes. In 1823 a fiery twenty-three-year-old Presbyterian minister, John Dunmore Lang, arrived with a colleague from Tasmania, as a further vexation to Marsden. Lang later publicly criticised him as exhibiting an 'episcopal intolerance' towards other Protestant denominations.

Non-Anglican Christian bodies in Australia were supported by Macquarie's successor, Thomas Brisbane, who became governor in 1821. He was a devout but broad minded Anglican who considered that the Catholic and Wesleyan Churches deserved government financial support. He baulked at giving financial assistance to Presbyterians, whom he regarded as wealthy enough to build their own churches. Nevertheless, the main support given by Brisbane and his successor, Ralph Darling, went to the Church of England in terms of land grants, clergy salaries and support for their schools. This was also the policy of Arthur, the first independent governor of Tasmania. He acknowledged the important work that Roman Catholics and Wesleyan Methodists were doing for the convicts and gave them financial support.

Government-supported Anglican schools at this stage provided most of the education for colonists. This was opposed by the Roman Catholic and Presbyterian churches, who saw it as financial support for an established church. However, these churches received support from Darling's successor, Richard Bourke. He was also an Anglican but was Irish-born and had Catholic friends and liberal principles. The consequence was the passing by the New South Wales Legislative Council of the 1836 *Church Act*. It provided for financial assistance for ministerial salaries and building subsidies to the four main denominations in Australia though, as the largest church, the Anglicans received the greatest share.

Such government support for the Christian churches did not transform the majority of European residents in Australia into church-goers. The first Anglican bishop in Australia, William Broughton, told Darling in 1830 that there were church seats for less than half of Sydney's Protestant population, and many of those were empty at Sunday worship services. In particular, members of the lower class showed 'little disposition to attend'.[9] By the 1840s, in the words of another contemporary observer, 'the lower orders especially ... have grown up in religious ignorance, and are but little susceptible of religious impressions'.[10] Only the Catholic Church retained major working class support. The close link between this church and the colony's Irish minority was encouraged by their minority status under Protestant domination. Also the first Catholic bishop in Australia, John Bede Polding, had a major concern to work personally among convicts and other poor Irish members of his diocese.

However, in Australia, despite widespread non-church attendance, there was still a dominant belief in God as a supreme being, reinforced by state, church and tradition. Consequently, in the 1828 census in New South Wales no colonist was listed as an atheist. Even the anti-clerical opponent of the Anglican ascendancy and advocate for self-government, William C. Wentworth, who campaigned in his *Australian* newspaper in 1824 for blowing away 'the sin, the smut, and the gloom of darkness of the parsons ... on gales of laughter and ridicule', later vigorously argued that his advocacy for a secular university would not promote atheism. On the contrary, university education would stimulate belief in 'the great Christian code'.[11] Few Europeans in early nineteenth-century Australia were as bold as William Nairne Clark in Western Australia, who claimed scandalously that 'he did not believe either in heaven or hell — in God or Devil'.[12] But private doubts were probably much greater. Also, a Sydney Anglican minister, Henry Fulton, was probably correct when he wrote in 1838 that even many church-goers expressed 'sentiments and affections with their lips to which their hearts were strangers'.[13]

Churches and moral order

The Church had difficulty in stamping its authority on moral behaviour and the use of Sundays in early Australia. Drunkenness was one of the greatest clergy complaints. Lang, when he arrived in 1823, was appalled at the excessive consumption of alcohol and considered the problem grew worse afterwards. He blamed high wages paid to workingmen, who were in short supply, especially those who were Irish. However, there was no Christian unanimity about a new remedy advocated by the temperance movement for the problem of liquor consumption. This program advocating individual abstinence from consumption of alcohol liquor, and aiming for its ultimate social prohibition, arrived in Australia from Britain in the 1830s. Temperance societies sprang up with tea-drinking meetings, children's 'cold water' parades and distribution of literature condemning the manifold evils of strong drink. They had some success with spreading abstinence pledges. Temperance attracted the support of clergy from all denominations, including some Catholic priests. However, high Anglican churchmen were suspicious of organisations outside their control and claimed that the temperance movement emphasised human endeavour rather than relying on divine grace. In 1836 Bishop Broughton exhibited his anti-temperance prejudice when, at a gathering to commemorate the second anniversary of the Diocesan Committee, he refused to agree that it was improper to celebrate with wine. In responding to a toast on behalf of the church, he prayed that the 'spirit of Puritanism' would never gain a foothold in New South Wales.[14] Such divisions in Christian ranks, irrespective of the penchant of many colonists for alcoholic drink, ensured no government acceptance of temperance objectives.

There was more Christian unanimity about the use of Sundays. There were frequent comments by clergymen in Sydney and Hobart about how Sundays were treated by many colonists as a day for entertainment or idleness rather than for church attendance. A Sydney minister denounced the 'prancing of horses and the rolling of chariots and the splashing of boat oars, and the revelry of parties, the disgusting ribaldry and profaneness of drunkenness', which were drowning out 'the songs of holy praise and joy'.[15] Broughton criticised Bourke for allowing the Sabbath to be treated by many as a drunken holiday. But when in 1840 he sought the banning of sporting events and sale of fresh meat on Sundays, the government and colonial establishment opposed this infringement of the liberties of colonists. The only concession by the Legislative Council was to prohibit the hunting of birds on Sundays. This noisy pastime had been a response to a craze for stuffed parrots, and it had aroused Broughton's attempt to impose a strict Sabbath on New South Wales.

Summary

This chapter has demonstrated that Christianity was largely rejected by convicts and by other working class Australians, except among the Irish minority. There was a growing alliance, if at times tenuous, between the Church of England and the state to impose moral order upon a licentious settler community. However, there was little community and government adherence to clergy efforts to impose strict sabbatarianism, and disagreement among clergy helped prevent the imposition of restrictions on the consumption of alcoholic liquor. The major state support for Christianity was government finance for the Church of England and for its near monopoly in education. But this government support aroused hostility from other denominations, especially Roman Catholics and Presbyterians, which helped prevent the Anglicans from becoming an established church. Though church-going was a minority activity in Australia, there was still an overall white community belief in God as a supreme being, which very few were willing to disavow openly. But there was a massive failure to persuade Aborigines to abandon their spirituality.

CHAPTER TWO

CHALLENGES TO PROTESTANT ASCENDANCY, *1840–1890*

The early establishment of state-supported Anglican dominance in the Christian presence in Australia came under increasing pressure from the 1840s. The major challenge occurred in the field of education. There were also other challenges from radical Protestants as well as Catholics to the close relationship between church and state. But many of those Protestants were concerned to use the state to increase church-dominated moral order, which was coming under threat by the 1880s. This chapter also considers the influence of Protestant-Catholic sectarian rivalry on colonial politics. It ends with discussions of the continued attempts by churches to convert Aborigines and Christian responses to the destruction of Aboriginal society.

Challenges to Anglican ascendancy in education

Along with his extension of the government's financial aid to non-Anglican denominations, Governor Bourke attempted to introduce government schools based on the national system in his native Ireland. The Irish system catered for a religiously divided country by having no denominational content, though allowing visiting clergy to teach their own children and with general religious content in the education program. However, non-Anglican Protestants, who had formed in 1835 a society for promoting schools where the Bible would be a basis for general education, insisted on its wider use in the proposed national schools than was allowed in the Irish system. Catholic support for Bourke's proposal further damned it in Protestant eyes. The consequent alliance between the Anglican and other Protestant denominations successfully banged an anti-Catholic drum to condemn concessions to a religious minority at the expense of Biblical-based religion in a national school system.

However, Bishop Broughton's hidden agenda included teaching the Anglican catechism. This agenda came into the open in 1839 when Governor Gipps proposed a Bible-based national system plus separate Catholic schools. Broughton successfully organised an agitation against this plan in favour of continued state support for Anglican schools, and other Protestants reacted by calling for government aid for their own educational programs. When a select committee of the New South Wales Legislative Council proposed the Irish system in 1846, Catholics, concerned that the schools could become agents of Protestant proselytisation, joined Anglicans and other Protestant denominations, especially Wesleyans, in opposing it. A compromise in 1848 agreed to separate denominational and Irish system-type national schools.

Catholic radicalism and Protestant conservatism

Some Catholics in early Australia provided a radical political challenge to the conservative Protestant establishment. This radicalism stemmed from increasing nationalist opposition to British rule in their Irish homeland, from Protestant persecution of Catholics in the early days of Australian settlement, and because of the working class status of a big majority of Australian Catholics. The Catholic press backed the campaign for full responsible government and for a democratic franchise. William Duncan, editor of the Catholic *Chronicle*, founded in 1839, was a strong supporter of radical anti-establishment causes and was supported by Bishop Polding. He later campaigned against squatters and the 'gentry' as editor of the independent *Weekly Register*. Meanwhile, the *Chronicle* continued to argue the causes of workingmen suffering from the 1840s depression and supported small farmers against the squatters. Catholics were prominent in the 'Australian' party in the New South Wales Legislative Council after 1848 and in the 'Australian' radical faction in Tasmania in the 1840s.

Another radical Catholic was Caroline Chisholm. She initially grew up in England under evangelical Anglican influence that encouraged her lifelong devotion to philanthropic causes. But she married a Catholic, converted to that faith, and championed the emigration of families to Australia. In the process of advocating and working personally to establish poor emigrants as a small farming class in the 1840s and, especially with her first-hand experiences with gold miners in Victoria in the 1850s, she influenced governments to support her causes such as the erection of wayside sheds for travelling miners. She also became a strong opponent of the squatting class and an advocate for universal suffrage, vote by ballot, and payment of members of parliament. This was a radical political agenda for the age. Another major contribution she made to Australian life was her devotion to the immigration of women in order to redress the imbalance of men and consequent social disorder. She saw female immigrants as 'God's police', who would bring new stability and order to Australia. Caroline Chisholm was a remarkable woman gaining unusual public fame and influence in England and Australia for her efforts on behalf of emigrants and miners in an age of male domination of churches and wider society.

By contrast, Anglican Bishop Broughton was a leader of Protestant conservatism. As a member of the Legislative Council until 1844, he opposed political reform, arguing for high property qualifications for voting. Many other Protestant leaders were also hostile to radical ideas. Presbyterian minister, John McGarvey, was a founder in 1831 and early leader writer of the *Sydney Morning Herald*, which from the start was a mouthpiece of Tory wealthy landowners. Its editor from 1854 to 1873, Congregationalist Minister, Timothy West, was a trenchant critic of the excesses of democracy. One of the few politically radical Australian Protestant ministers, John Dunmore Lang, declared in 1857 that 'the clergy of all communions, especially if supported by the State, are almost uniformly on the side of wealth, and rank, and power, and ... hate universal suffrage'.[1]

Radical Protestants

Lang, who was constantly re-elected to the New South Wales Legislature as the champion of the common people, advocated full democracy, payment of members of parliament, and equality of opportunity for all. He was a maverick in the early New South Wales Protestant community. He formed his own Presbyterian Synod as a protest against state support for the church, which had been accepted by McGarvey whom Lang later castigated as 'a worshipper of the god Mammon'.[2] A prominent Anglican laymen, Chief Justice Sir Alfred Stephen, imposed the conservative colonial establishment's censure of Lang's strident criticisms by sentencing him to four months' imprisonment for libel in 1851. Lang's later political diatribes against West extended to mutual libel suits.

The Australian colony experiencing the most radical Protestant influence was South Australia. In this colony, where non-Anglican Protestantism was by far the strongest — 52% of the population in 1860 — some Christians were in the forefront of social and political reform movements. John Stephens, founder of a Methodist journal in England, became the first editor in 1843 of one of the colony's main newspapers, *The South Australian Register*, which advocated civil and religious liberty. In 1848 he earned the wrath of copper mine owners by supporting striking miners. Prominent nonconformists supported universal suffrage. They also pushed for the voluntary principle of no state aid for religion as a means of escaping Anglican domination. These radical opinions were grounded in the earlier discrimination against nonconformism in England and the linkage there of religious emancipation with political reform. Among the conservative opponents of reform there were prominent Anglicans, such as Robert Torrens, who claimed that full scale democracy would introduce an 'oligarchy of democrats'. Furthermore, some nonconformists, such as the philanthropic entrepreneur, George Angas, successfully supported property qualifications for the upper house in the South Australian Parliament.

There was broad support among non-Anglican Protestants in South Australia for the voluntary principle in church-state relations. This issue was linked to democratic progress by supporters of voluntarism and became a major line of political division in the 1851 colonial election, with victory in eleven of the sixteen elective seats to the voluntarists. Consequently, state aid to churches in South Australia was abolished. In education, government aid was granted only to schools which gave 'good secular instruction, based on the Christian religion, apart from all theological and controversial differences on discipline and doctrine'.[3] This colony had agreed upon the first system of secular education based on a common Christianity in Australia. But the small minority of Catholics rejected it and started their own school system.

Protestant moral order

Nevertheless, many nonconformists in South Australia still wished to use the state to impose a moral order on the Australian people. One was a Wesleyan Methodist layman, John Colton, a leader of the anti-state aid campaign who became Premier of South Australia from 1876 to 1877. He and other Methodists, who were the strongest non-Anglican Protestant group in South Australia, concentrated on transforming individual South Australians into more moral persons by raising the age of sexual consent, by promoting abstinence from alcoholic drink, by preventing them from wasting money in gambling, and by maintaining a sabbatarian Sunday, which had been imposed to the extent of locking children's swings on Saturday nights. It was a holy crusade. Methodists were exhorted to always vote at elections as 'a solemn trust' to ensure true Christian influence in Parliament.[4]

In the neighbouring new colony of Victoria there was a similar transformation of Protestant political reformers into moral crusaders. One of the most important early radical liberals in Victoria was George Higinbotham. He was an Irish born Anglican lawyer, who was a prominent member of the Victorian Legislative Assembly until appointed to the bench of the Victorian Supreme Court in 1880. His championship of equal rights for rich and poor was deeply grounded in his strong religious conviction of the equality of all God's people. But in the 1870s he became a leader of the movement for legislation to allow local councils to ban the sale of alcoholic drink — called local option — which prompted the *Argus's* weekly journal, the *Australasian*, to brand him 'an infallible Pope' bent on establishing a 'moral dictatorship'. His aim was to remove the 'thraldom' of liquor and gambling on working men.[5]

One consequence of this crusade was a struggle in Victoria in the 1880s between moral Protestant reformers and a growing coalition of opponents. A major battleground was pressure to break down previous sabbatarian laws by opening the Melbourne Public Library, the Technological Museum and the National Art Gallery on Sundays. On this issue Christians divided. Leading Anglicans and Catholics and a prominent Presbyterian minister, the Rev. Charles Strong, joined Higinbotham and more secular minded liberal intellectuals, with the support of Victoria's two leading morning newspapers, the *Argus* and the *Age*, to campaign for the opening of these halls of learning and culture for the working class people of the colony. There was a strong reaction from most evangelical Protestants. The Presbyterian Assembly organised a 'very large deputation' to call on the Premier, James Service, to urge the sanctity of the Christian Sabbath. This issue dwarfed all others at the time in the convening of meetings, in letters to newspaper editors, and in petitions to Parliament. But though 36000 petitioners for Sunday opening outnumbered their opponents, the sabbatarians had the numbers in Parliament. Service was a lapsed Presbyterian, but many of his Cabinet colleagues were staunch evangelical churchmen who were able to keep the library, gallery and museum closed on Sundays well into the next century.

Nevertheless, there were limits to the degree of evangelical Protestant control of the Victorian community. Temperance reform was limited. The case for liquor reform was strong, with a hotel or beer shop for every 225 people in Victoria and unrestricted sales of alcohol by grocers. Hotels could open from 6 a.m to midnight and often breached a law banning Sunday trading passed in 1854. Pushing for reform in the 1880s were numerous temperance societies in Victoria influenced by visiting British and American temperance crusaders and supported by many members of the non-Anglican Protestant churches plus some Anglicans. Opposed to them were the vested interests of brewers and hostelers, government fearfulness of losing excise revenue, and popular opposition to the moral-police pretensions of evangelicals. When the government responded to the evangelical pressure with new liquor legislation, the gains were small: half an hour earlier closing for hotels, a reduction in their number, and a local option system which required one-third of the electors to cast a vote for a valid poll. The voting stipulation was difficult to achieve, and liquor interests found loopholes in the laws to stop hotels closing.

Evangelicals in New South Wales had a harder task than their Victorian colleagues to stop the erosion of sabbatarian Sundays. By 1880, most Sydney people were using Sunday as a day of entertainment as well as rest. Evangelical Protestants, who established in 1880 the Lord's Day Observance Society, were unable to persuade Parliament to rescind a motion passed in 1878 to open the public library and museum on Sunday afternoons. In 1882 a nominal Anglican, Henry Copeland, who depended on working class electoral support, succeeded against Premier Henry Parkes's opposition, with a motion passed to open the new art gallery as well on Sunday afternoons. A new government headed by high Anglican churchman, Alexander Stuart, resisted further evangelical pressure to ban Sunday afternoon concerts. He suggested to the deputationists from the Lord's Day Observance Society that they were out of step with public opinion.

Secular education

The primary Protestant-Catholic political battleground was education. Victoria inherited initially from New South Wales the dual system of state-supported dominational and 'national' schools. The curriculum contained significant Christian teaching, and visiting clergy were allowed to instruct children of their denomination. Catholics, with their concern about Protestant domination of these schools moved to set up their own non-state supported school system and were assisted by vigorous recruitment of teaching brothers and nuns from religious orders in Europe.

Initially, the close alliance between Protestant churches and the Victorian Government tipped the balance against the national schools. However, the rapid gold-driven expansion of Victoria's population was producing strains on the churches' ability to maintain their schools, and there were questions about the quality of education. Also, the manifest difficulty of deciding on a non-denominational religious agenda in this age of strong religious doctrinal disputes encouraged Higinbotham to support a push by a small group of rationalist secularists to remove any religious instruction from the national system. He received enough support from Protestants, including some Anglicans, who were prepared to back a secular system in return for the cessation of state aid to denominational schools and the establishment of a strong state system of education in the cause of government responsibility for the establishment of a common citizenship. Even the Anglican Archbishop, Charles Perry, eventually supported secular education because he regarded non-denominational teaching as too watered down to be of any use. The Victorian *Education Act* of 1872 introduced the most secular school system in Australia. Religious education in those schools could take place only after school hours with the permission of local boards. Nevertheless, school children were expected each week to pledge their loyalty to God as well as to Queen Victoria and the British Empire.

Sectarian politics

Catholic rivalry with Protestants had an influence in Victorian colonial politics. In the first election in Victoria in 1856 state aid for religion was a significant issue, with voluntarist opposition among many non-Anglican Protestants and strong support for government finance to religion by Catholics, who constituted a fifth of the Victorian community. A leading Catholic, the formerly prominent Irish nationalist politician, Charles Gavin Duffy, rightly claimed that 'the no popery cry was employed at the ... general election to the largest extent practicable'. Certainly, most of the elected Catholics represented areas of large Catholic population. But they also needed significant Protestant support, which prompted Duffy also to aver that 'the good sense of the community defeated' the sectarian campaign.[6] Indeed, the Irish Catholic John O'Shanassy was Premier in 1857–59 and 1861–63.

Duffy was a leader of radical opinion in Parliament, but his Catholic religion made it difficult for Protestant liberals to cooperate with him. Indeed, there had been an intense Protestant political campaign against him and other Catholics exploiting the alleged designs by the Roman Pope to reconquer the Protestant world. While much of the propaganda was spurious, the Pope had contributed to the problem by issuing in 1864 his Syllabus of Errors, which denounced the western world-wide liberal political agenda, and by the declaration in 1870 of Papal infallibility.

Nevertheless, in 1871 Duffy became Premier, leading a radical liberal government with Graham Berry, a nominal Anglican, as his chief deputy. But a stronger Catholic push for a separate education system gave conservative opponents of the Duffy Government's radical program, such as government control of the railways, increased opportunity to employ anti-Catholic propaganda against him. They achieved the Duffy Government's defeat before the end of the year. With only 24% of Victoria's population in 1881, Catholics were not politically strong enough to relaize their aim of achieving state aid for their schools without Protestant cooperation, which was not forthcoming.

There was similar sectarian rivalry in New South Wales politics. Major political leadership for the national school system there was provided by Henry Parkes. He had been a regular worshipper at a Congregational chapel in Birmingham, but was never deeply committed to Christianity. Nevertheless, he had imbibed an identity between Protestantism and social progress, which informed a growing hostility to perceived anti-progressive Catholicism. He made valuable political mileage from the education issue. As Colonial Secretary in the government of James Martin, an Irish Catholic whose social ambitions had caused him to become a fellow traveller with Anglicans, Parkes introduced in 1866 a *Public Schools Act*. It placed both the national and denominational systems under a Council of Education, which would supervise teacher training and the content of secular education in all schools. In the state's public schools visiting clergy could give denominational religious instruction, and the common Christianity of the Irish national system would be incorporated into regular teaching. The Catholic Church demanded full control of its own schools, and its most extreme members led a bitter attack against Parkes's 'godless' proposal. Parkes made no effort to assuage their anger in a sectarian controversy that assured him extra votes from the Protestant majority.

The political potency of anti-Catholicism was increased in 1868 when in Sydney a paranoiac Irish nationalist, Henry O'Farrell, shot and wounded visiting Prince Alfred, the Duke of Edinburgh. Parkes talked darkly about a non-existent Fenian plot, though this was promoted as much by genuine fear as by political opportunism. Many members of Orange Lodges, which assiduously stoked in Australia the fires of Northern Irish anti-Catholicism, plus other chauvinistic Protestants joined in the anti-Catholic agitation. They included Lang, who warned that New South Wales would be transformed 'into a mere province of the Popedom'.[7]

However, New South Wales politics were not long divided on sectarian lines. Parkes, who resigned from the government in 1868 and from Parliament in 1870 when he descended into bankruptcy, was quite happy to make a secret political pact with an influential Catholic politician, Edward Butler. Their target was the governing coalition of James Martin and John Robertson, who had been a member of the radical Protestant political coalition in the 1850s, but who was able to balance membership of Freemasonry, a Protestant secret society, with sympathy for the aspirations of the Irish National League and support for the Catholic campaign against Parkes's education bill. In the 1872 election campaign, while Butler attacked Martin as a renegade Catholic, Parkes vilified Robertson. This unholy alliance gained enough votes to elevate Parkes to the premiership. Butler was rewarded with the post of Attorney-General.

Parkes, leading another ministry in 1879, pushed through a Public Instruction Bill, which abolished state aid to denominational schools to match a previous abolition of other state aid to religion. Catholics were outraged, but Butler had been involved in the original framing of the education bill. New South Wales had caught up with South Australia, Victoria, and the other Australian colonies in the implementation of a free, compulsory, and secular state school system.

Challenges to Christian ascendancy

There were increased secularist challenges to Christianity by the 1880s. Free-thinking opposition to Christianity was strongest in the most populous and cosmopolitan colony, Victoria. One prominent group was the Victorian Association of Progressive Spiritualists, who rejected the unscientific nature of the Bible, especially the alleged depravity of human beings, and the threat of eternal damnation. Inheriting ideas from a wave of spiritualism in the United States and Western Europe, they had a gnostic view of the perfectibility of human beings. According to one of their early Australian leaders, G. S. Manns: 'man is an eternally progressive being'.[8] They believed that science proved the existence of God and that human beings could align themselves to his purpose by studying his scientific laws. They also tried to turn séances into scientific experiments. Their most famous member in the 1880s was the Australian-born young politician and future Australian Prime Minister, Alfred Deakin. Most were former non-Anglican Protestants, influenced by Protestant individualism. But spiritualists in Victoria were never more than 1500 strong; and they were bedevilled by internal disputes.

More strident opponents of Christianity were secularists belonging to groups such as the Sunday Free Discussion Society of the 1870s and the Australasian Secular Association, founded in 1882 with a charter proclaiming that only science could promote human happiness. Chief spokesman of these free thinkers was Joseph Symes, a renegade Wesleyan minister from England, who travelled through Melbourne and the Victorian countryside in the mid-1880s giving impressive public lectures laced with virulent attacks on the alleged fallacies and immoralities of Christianity and praising the glories of free thought. His program included Sunday morning secular 'services'.

Evangelicals placed intense pressure on the Victorian Government to silence Symes. The government did not hesitate to try to defend Christianity from such virulent attacks. Knowing that a charge of blasphemy was unlikely to succeed, Symes was charged under an English Act preventing admission fees for public entertainments on Sundays. His defence was that his was another denomination.

Although Chief Justice Higinbotham condemned his 'gross and outrageous insults upon the faith of a large section of the community', two juries failed to come to a decision. So the government abandoned its case, and Symes was free to continue his campaign. However, his appeal weakened after 1886 due to the stridency of his anti-Christian propaganda, the significant community opposition which he faced, such as banning him from lecture halls, and the divisions in secularist ranks.

In Sydney, the emergence of 'free thought lectures' on Sundays in the 1880s brought pressure on Parkes from a new evangelical Sydney Ministers' Union formed to achieve a ban on these lectures and other Sabbath-breaking activities. Though he refused to bow to the sabbatarian aim, Parkes closed down the theatres holding 'blasphemous' lectures as offending the Christian majority in the community. The Sydney *Bulletin*, founded in 1880 by two liberal-minded Catholics and given an anti-clerical bent by its radically minded second principal owner and editor, William Henry Traill, denounced Parkes as toadying to the Protestant clergy, which it constantly depicted as wowsers and kill-joys. However, Parkes knew that in suppressing the secularists he enjoyed majority public support.

Indeed, very few citizens of the Australian colonies were prepared to deny any attachment to Christianity or another religion in the 1891 census. The 8571 Victorians who declared they had 'no religion' were only 0.75% of the population. South Australia had the highest number denying any religion — 2.7% — possibly a symptom of the early secularisation of education there. In the new colony of Queensland, where there were nearly 18 000 Buddhists and pagans because of big Chinese goldmining and Pacific Islander labourer (Kanaka) communities, the avowed atheists were 1.3% of the population. In 1891, another 2% of Australia's population objected to stating their religion or did not answer the religious question, signs of the pervasive Christian influence that made atheists and agnostics unwilling to express an opinion. Acknowledged Christians that year were 95% of Australia's non-Aboriginal population. Jews were 0.4%. Aborigines were not counted. Parkes could rightly claim in 1880 that Australians 'are pre-eminently a Christian people'.[9]

In fact, Christianity had increased its personal influence in Australia since the middle of the century. Christian church attendance rates had risen. In Victoria in 1890 43% of the population attended churches each Sunday. In South Australia, the estimated attendance rate in the

1880s was 40%. The Victorian attendance represented a high two-thirds of the population of over fourteen years of age. Overall, the more than 40% proportion of regular worshippers in those two colonies was higher than contemporary Sunday attendance in Britain.[10] By contrast, in New South Wales Sunday church attendances were only 27% of the population in 1890.

It was perhaps significant that church attendance was higher in the colonies less affected by the convict origins of early European settlement. Many of the settlers arriving in South Australia and Victoria had been influenced by the evangelical revival in British Protestantism in the first half of the nineteenth century and had a more middle class base than the convict-influenced early Australian population. The relatively high church attendance in the 1880s was also a tribute to the strong energy applied to church expansion, especially by Methodists. They benefited from a popular revivalist tradition, from the use of lay preachers to cover shortages of clergy, and from prolific church building influenced by competition among the different branches of Methodism. The lusty hymn singing of Methodist worship services and the community-creating organisation of their church life also attracted people from other denominations. Together, the Methodist denominations had the highest average church attendance of any major denomination.

Churches still had major roles to play in Australian society. In many homes grace was said before meals and there was a general belief in an omniscient God who could bring floods and droughts to sinful people, causing people to flock to special services offering prayers for better times. At times of great disasters, such as shipwrecks and colliery explosions, clergy were prominent and welcomed in the prayer and solace they could offer to sorrowing people. In this age before radio and cinema, churches were major centres of entertainment with concerts and other musical events. In country towns, such as Castlemaine in central Victoria, the churches organised children into Sunday Schools. Mechanics institutes were founded for working class adult 'improving' education, and the churches maintained a firm control of the community's ritual life: birth, marriage and death.[11] Even in the 1880s in Sydney and Melbourne a secular funeral was a rarity and a scandal.

The ethnic flavour of the churches provided a welcoming community for immigrants, such as Irish Catholics, Scottish Presbyterians, Cornish Methodists and German Lutherans. These immigrants brought their religious disputes to Australia. Methodists established Wesleyan, Primitive Methodist, Bible Christian, New Connection, and United Free Methodist chapels and churches. There were Presbyterian and Free Presbyterian churches and two branches of Lutheranism. Cemeteries were rigidly segregated into religious zones, but patterns of settlement much less so. In the big cities Catholics were not segregated residentially as in Liverpool in England, though they were more prominent in inner working class suburbs. There were also marriages between the single men and women who made up much of the Irish immigration with Protestants, to the extent that Catholic bishops moved to stop the practice. Evangelical Christianity, especially, encouraged private virtues of thrift, hard work and individual responsibility, enabling poor immigrants to 'improve' themselves.

However, by the 1880s Christian churches in Australia were facing wider challenges than attacks by secularists. The Darwinist theory of evolution had become a major challenge to the evangelical faith that was held by most Anglicans and other Protestants. Biblical criticism also was testing fundamentalist views of the Bible. While many ministers and lay people shrugged off the new ideas, they were producing doubts and divisions among some, especially educated people. Also the resistance of many evangelicals to new environmental and liberal ideas were fuelling the arguments of the secularists. Higinbotham was one Christian intellectual who rejected the organised churches because of their stifling of free thought.

Indeed, a lecture Higinbotham gave on science and religion in August 1883 precipitated a serious rift in the Presbyterian church between the evangelical majority and one of its liberal ministers, Charles Strong, who chaired the meeting. He was already under a cloud in his presbytery for the liberal nature of his preaching (which included outspoken attacks on social evils), for his rejection of the fundamentalist seventeenth-century Westminster confession, and for his opposition to sabbatarianism. He was threatened with a charge of heresy for not disassociating himself from Higinbotham's views. Though strongly supported by the majority of members of his parish, the prestigious Scots Church in Melbourne, Strong preferred to leave the colony for Scotland in November 1883 on the day before he was expelled from the Presbyterian Church. However, he returned to Victoria a year later and established the non-doctrinal Australian church with the support of many of his former Scots Church parishioners and other religious liberals.

Christians and the working class

Only the Catholic Church had any significant following among working class Australians who, in the 1880s, were as much alienated from Protestant churches as in the convict era. One reason for this was a lack of attention to poor urban areas in the big church expansion which occurred in the third quarter of the century. During the Strong controversy, his Scots Church supporters produced a petition from the 'inhabitants of the lowest lanes and alleys of the city' which said: 'Many of us had sunk very low in vice, misery and crime when Mr Strong found us out. No city missionary or minister of religion ever visited our dwellings'.[12] In Sydney in 1881 and 1884 Protestant clergymen were warned that their church worship 'had signally failed' to attract working class people and that children of slum dwellers were growing up believing 'that churches and ministers were all very well for rich people, but could have nothing to do with them'.[13]

Exceptions to the normal pattern were some of the socially cohesive mining communities influenced by Primitive Methodism, which had significant influence among workers, especially miners, in England. A prominent example was Broken Hill, where many miners had arrived from Cornwall and Northumbria, regions of Methodist strength, to mine rich lodes of silver, nickel and zinc. Miners predominated among the people who attended morning services in the Primitive Methodist Blende Street church, which extended its seating capacity to 450 in 1888. There were smaller numbers of miners in the Bible Christian and Wesleyan Methodist churches. However, in this booming mining town at the end of 1888 all Christian churches had seating accommodation for less than one-fifth of the town's population of over 10 000. Also its fifty-five hotels were strong competition for the Methodist majority of the town's worshippers; and the law that had prohibited Sunday opening of hotels was breached more than it was observed.[14]

It is true that by the 1880s Protestants in the big metropolitan cities were waking up to their lack of influence among the poor who had been regarded as morally responsible for their own poverty. But the negative nature of the church's movements against alcohol and gambling was repulsive to people whose poor living conditions encouraged such escapist activities. Evangelical attempts in the 1880s to clean up the uncontrolled prostitution in Melbourne in previous decades by exposing landlords and owners of brothels, by organising refuges for 'fallen' sisters, and by seeking anti-prostitution legislation, failed. Too many men in respectable Melbourne society were involved as entrepreneurs or clients of the industry. The only effect was that it became less open, but with no evident decline in the number of prostitutes or brothels.

In Sydney in the 1880s evangelical reformers attempted to clean up the squalor and vice they saw abounding among the 'lower orders' of the city. Volunteers from the New South Wales Temperance Society and the Sydney City Mission distributed religious tracts, gave 'good' advice, and organised Sunday schools for children. In the inner suburbs of Sydney, where population densities had more than doubled between 1871 and 1891, there was much overcrowded, badly ventilated, ill-drained and decaying housing. Consequently, there were attempts by middle class Christians to sanitise working class living areas and to rehouse the poor. But the small minority of Christians doing this work lacked wider community support. The emphasis was also on inculcating middle class values in the 'lower orders'. In the 1880s there was only slow progress towards the realisation among reformers and politicians that government action was needed to make any major difference to the overcrowded housing in inner suburbs of Sydney.

The Australian Catholic Church also imbibed some of the dominant Protestant attitudes to moral respectability. Catholic priests generally did not support sabbatarianism and the temperance movement but had similar attitudes to sexual morality as bourgeois Protestants and deplored cultural developments such as ballroom dancing. In part, Catholics were concerned to be no less morally respectable than their Protestant competitors. Many Irish descendants wanted to escape their convict and working class origins. But there was less unbending moral disapproval in the Catholic Church's attitudes to sinners and their sins, which was associated with the central roles of confession and the saving grace of the sacraments. There was also more Catholic clerical acceptance of the often rowdy behaviour of many working class parishioners.

Indeed, much of the non-Catholic response to the poor in Australia in the 1880s came from outside the mainline Protestant denominations. The Salvation Army was a disciplined and energetic group, arriving in Australia in the 1880s in direct response to the church's neglect of the poor. Though this new denomination brought an evangelistic approach concentrating on saving sinners for Christ, the willingness of its members to live among the poor and deliver social services to them won some adherents, though many of these were drawn from other churches. By the end of the 1880s this strange group of Christians with their martial uniforms and loud music had earned the grudging respect of other Christians.

Unitarians, who had rejected personal Christian faith, were also more likely than mainline Protestants to involve themselves in catering for the needs of disadvantaged people. In Adelaide two Unitarian women, Emily Clark and Catherine Helen Spence, were devoting much energy in the 1870s and 1880s to providing foster care for homeless children. It was significant that, in the Unitarian offshoot from male-dominated Christianity, women were more in the forefront of reform, though they were wedded to the ideal of raising working class children to middle class values. In 1886 Strong's Australian Church in Melbourne established the Social Improvement Friendly Help and Children's Aid Society to operate in the working class suburbs of Collingwood and Fitzroy. This Society founded creches for working mothers.

There were some attempts in mainline churches to reach out to the alienated poor. A prominent example was the Central Methodist Mission founded in Sydney in 1884 by William George Taylor, who revived the nearly empty York Street Church with street preaching, brass bands, gaudy advertising, and musical items in worship services. But many Methodists were scandalised by such unorthodox methods, and among their minority of working class members few were manual labourers. This situation in Australia matched the social composition of churches in England and in the United States. 'Go into an ordinary church on Sunday morning', declared an American Protestant clergyman in 1887, 'and you will see lawyers, physicians, merchants, and business men with their families ... but the workingman and his household are not there'.[15]

However, in their emphasis on 'respectability' and moral order, churches — Protestant and Catholic — had contributed to falling crime rates in Australia compared with the convict past. Admittedly, the earlier image of a 'vicious society' held by middle class people in New South Wales was greater than the actuality. Also the lawlessness of a frontier society and an excess of males in the early population contributed to crime rates that peaked in the 1830s. The crime rate in New South Wales then declined steadily, with some humps, for the rest of the century — from 1077 convictions in higher courts per 100 000 people in 1835 to under 100 by 1890. There were similar, though less steep, rates of decline in higher court convictions in the other colonies from their early years to 1890.[16]

Furthermore, even though many working class people had no active contact with the church, there was still among most a residual belief in God. A Methodist evangelist, Henry Hall, who in 1884 started tramping the streets of the Melbourne working class suburb of Prahran, found few people who expressed 'very peculiar views' by denying the sovereignty of God.[17]

Continued Aboriginal resistance to Christianity

In the 1840s two of Australia's most enterprising church leaders, Lang and Polding, had been trying to bridge the yawning gap between Christianity and the Aboriginal inhabitants of Australia. To avoid the Sydney region, where there were corrupting influences on Aborigines — none of whom had become Christians — Lang and Polding chose an area of new settlement, Moreton Bay in the future colony of Queensland. But they also sent there missionaries from continental Europe because of the shortage of available clergy in Australia. Lang arranged for a team of lay and clerical German Lutherans to set up a self-supporting mission at Moreton Bay. Polding sent four Italian Passionate priests.

These missionaries were no more successful than their predecessors. The Lutherans quickly developed a contempt for Aboriginal culture, and disputes emerged between themselves and with Aborigines, who had no concept of the alienation of the land that the missionaries farmed. The Catholic Italian missionaries soon concluded that Aboriginal adults were beyond redemption and, in a departure from normal Catholic practice, they refused to baptise the children of non-believers. They bemoaned the corrupting influences of the growing white settlement in the region but also demanded police protection. When giving evidence in 1845 to a Parliamentary Select Committee on the Condition of the Aborigines, Polding explained the main reason for the lack of missionary success among Australian Aborigines:

> the bad feeling and want of confidence, naturally caused by the mode in which possession has been taken of their country — occupation by force, accompanied by murders, ill-treatment, ravishment of their women, in a

word, to the conviction on their minds that the white man has come for his own advantage, without any regard to their rights.[18]

Such prescience was rare in the contemporary Australian European community.

Nor were Christians able to stop the wanton destruction of Aborigines and their society. In Victoria, a staunchly Presbyterian pastoralist, Niel Black, who abhorred intemperance and was fastidious about keeping the Sabbath, was concerned about being involved in the shooting of Aborigines. Race relations had already been infected by the settlers who imported into Victoria the revolting practices imposed on Tasmanian Aborigines; by the common settler feelings of racial superiority, which depicted the Aborigines as 'savages' at the bottom of the racial pecking order; and by the economic advancement motives which brushed aside the evangelical-influenced concern of the British Government and Governor Gipps to protect the Aborigines. The execution of the Myall Creek murderers had merely made the rampant shooting of Aborigines in Victoria more secretive and had substituted poisoning of food for bullets. Black was well aware of this European savagery perpetrated by his fellow settlers. 'Two thirds of them', he wrote, 'does not care a single straw about taking the life of natives'.[19] He therefore made sure that he bought in 1840 an established pastoral run in the Western District, where the task of clearing away local Aborigines had been completed. But though he tried to avoid killing Aborigines, he destroyed Aboriginal huts discovered on his property, and he fired over the heads of Aborigines found hunting for food on his land. Like others, his drive to make profits induced him to participate in the general destruction of Aboriginal society in Victoria.

Christian 'successes' with Aborigines

Indeed Christianity, still firmly clad in the garb of European 'civilization', was not imposed on Aborigines until they were cowed into submission by the destruction wrought by white settlers. Mass murder was accompanied by introduced diseases, not only epidemics such as smallpox, measles and influenza, but also venereal diseases introduced by the widespread exploitation of Aboriginal women by European men. The effect of this devastation upon Aboriginal acceptance of Christianity was first observed in Victoria as its fertile land was rapidly taken over by pastoralists during the 1840s. Then in the next decade there was a gold rush-engendered boom in the white population. Aborigines were left with few areas in which their life style could survive. The result was that some were willing to accept the protection of mission stations and at least outwardly conform to Christianity as a price to be paid for mission support.

A prominent case was the Ebenezer mission in Victoria's Wimmera River district. Its founders were two German missionaries, Willhelm Spieseke and Friedrich Hagenauer of the Moravian faith which had a long history of enthusiasm for overseas missions. These two missionaries were supported by the local pastoralist, a Belgian immigrant Horatio Ellerman, who in 1858 gave them a piece of his land to erect the mission. He had earned a fearsome reputation for the savagery with which he had cleared Aborigines from his property. He also was a prominent Presbyterian churchman, who was perhaps repenting for previous sins by now strongly supporting the new mission. Furthermore, his past played a role when the missionaries, after banning corroborees, were confronted by angry blacks. A timely arrival by the feared Ellerman stopped a potential armed attack on the mission camp. Gradually, some adults were encouraged to become permanent residents at the station and allow their children to attend the mission school. In 1860 one of the boys, named Pepper, was baptised and given the Christian name Nathaniel. He was widely proclaimed as the first Aboriginal Christian, and while there were predecessors, his was the first publicised conversion.

In 1862 Hagenauer moved to Gippsland, where Aborigines had been decimated by warfare with settlers and by subsequent intertribal fighting provoked by competition for depleted land resources. His mission station, named Ramahyuck at Lake Wellington, became a tightly organised village under his despotic control. He showed his contempt for Aboriginal culture by burning spears and boomerangs. He also became an official, and for a time, the secretary of the government's Board of Protection of Aborigines. In that position, Hagenauer influenced the draconian Victorian *Aborigines Protection Act* of 1886, which separated all half-caste children and young adults from mission stations. He thereby created great personal consternation by breaking up the many families into which European blood had been introduced by the rapes, abductions and general sexual exploitation of Aboriginal women.

A different and more successful approach to the Christianising of Aborigines was the Catholic mission established by Dom Rosendo

Salvado in the Victoria Plains of Western Australia, about 100 kilometres northeast of Perth. Arriving from Spain into this fertile region in 1846, Salvado with his brother monk Dom Joseph Serra and a few helpers, had so few resources that they had to plough the land themselves and in bare feet. Their obvious lack of wealth and their willingness to do all menial tasks for themselves impressed local Aborigines, who were soon providing them with food. By 1847, with the assistance of money raised at a piano concert in Perth given by the musically-gifted Salvado, the monks built a monastery and named it 'New Norcia', around which gathered a large number of Aborigines. In the same year the mission conducted its first baptism of an Aborigine, and the government granted the mission extensive property. Salvado also gained British citizenship in 1848. This allowed him to defend Aborigines in court against false charges of sheep-stealing, further enhancing his status among the local community.

However, in 1849 Salvado received 'terrible news', while on a visit back to Spain, that the Pope had appointed him bishop of Port Victoria (Port Essington) in the Northern Territory. He rightly considered this would make him 'quite isolated' from New Norcia.[20] He had to plead his cause in Rome, and with continuing correspondence when he returned to Australia, before the Vatican in 1859 confirmed his appointment to New Norcia as head of an abbey independent of diocesan control. With the help of other monks, he made the abbey financially secure and not dependant on Aboriginal labour as with Protestant missions. The mission was run for Aborigines. Though wanting to civilise them, Salvado took a much more lenient attitude to their culture than did his Protestant counterparts, allowing them to hunt for food, to retain other traditional skills, and to settle as they wished on the abbey's land. The Protestant-owned *Perth Gazette* complained that New Norcia's Aborigines were not really Christians because they did not live like Europeans. Salvado had avoided the marriage between European culture and Christianity which had bedevilled Protestant missionary work among Aborigines.

Nevertheless, there were limits to Salvado's influence on the future of Western Australia's Aborigines. It has been estimated that he came into contact with no more than 700 of them.[21] Also numbers declined as time progressed with the thinning of the Aboriginal population in the region under the impact of spreading European settlement.

Furthermore, when it came to a contest in Western Australia in the 1880s between employers of Aboriginal labour and a vociferous missionary critic, the capitalists won a major victory. Their opponent was an Anglican priest, John Gribble, who had founded a mission for Aborigines in New South Wales. In 1885 he was invited by Bishop Henry Parry of Perth, to establish a mission in the Gascoyne River region of Western Australia, which had been settled since the 1860s by whites engaged in pearling and pastoral activities. Parry recognised that 'very little had been done to bring [the Aborigines of his colony] into a better condition'.[22] The outspoken Gribble soon declared in the introduction to his 1886 pamphlet, *Dark Deeds in a Sunny Land*, that Australia had 'become the theatre of the dark deeds of oppression and cruelty'.[23] He demonstrated the accusation with details of rampant sexual exploitation of Aboriginal women and mistreatment of Aboriginal labourers, which he had observed in three months of travel in the Gascoyne district. The book aroused a furore of opposition from the employers of the region and their capitalist allies in Perth. The Anglican mission committee and the Dean of Perth Cathedral, with Parry absent from the colony, responded by banning Gribble from preaching in Carnarvon and Perth. The colony's major daily newspaper, the *West Australian*, co-edited by a member of the Anglican mission committee, accused Gribble of 'lying, canting humbug'. Gribble's riposte of a writ for £10 000 damages for libel became a *cause célèbre* in Perth. During the trial there were unguarded admissions, such as by George Bush, an Anglican and Gascoyne pastoralist, that he had heard of natives 'being run down and unlawfully taken ... and chained up' and that he had sent Aboriginal women to sleep with his white stockmen. Nevertheless, the two presiding judges, in a closing of the elite ranks of the colony, delivered a verdict in favour of the newspaper.

Summary

This chapter has demonstrated that the challenges by Catholics and secularists had not removed the Protestant ascendancy. Indeed, Protestant church attendance had increased by the 1880s. Also minority Catholics needed Protestant support in politics which limited the degree of influence of sectarian politics in Victoria and New South Wales, the colonies with big Catholic communities. However, in the struggle over education systems Catholics had established their own school system and most Protestants had supported a secular state system with limited scope for religious instruction. This sowed future seeds of secularist indifference to Christianity. That challenge was present by the 1880s with the emergence of Australians for the first time willing to declare their atheism. But the percentage was minute. Australia was still nominally a Christian country. However, there were differences among the Christian community about how much governments should enforce Protestant moral values as in the controversies about sabbatarianism. There were also limits to the degree to which the churches could impose moral standards, demonstrated by the limited inroads of the temperance movement. The negative nature of Protestant social and moral concern helped keep the 'lower orders' alienated from all but Catholicism, with the exception of the advent of the Salvation Army. Most Protestant clergy were politically conservative, as were many actively religious politicians. Protestant reformers were also concentrating on symptoms rather than causes of social evils, though there was the beginning of an approach to improving working class living conditions by a small minority of reformers. There was also an expansion of 'respectable society' as demonstrated by the fall in crime rates.

Aborigines had strongly resisted Protestant cultural imperialism, with only the Catholic Salvado making some headway by accepting Aboriginal customs. Not until Aborigines were cowed by the rapacity of white society, did some accept Protestant paternalism. Also the few Christians who protested about abuses of Aboriginal rights were unable to prevail against churches and society dominated by capitalist and racist values.

CHAPTER THREE

SOCIAL JUSTICE AND MORAL ORDER, *1890–1914*

The 1890s ushered in an era of deep depression in Australia, which provided a challenge to the social conscience of the churches. One of the depression's symptoms was the way employers were able to use unemployed workers to crush opposition from emerging trade unions pushing for a 'closed shop' for unionists and the raising of low wages. The support given by State governments to the employers convinced unions to turn to a political solution: the formation of a Labor Party to influence governments in favour of workers' rights. This chapter discusses the reactions of the churches to industrial turmoil and to the emerging Labor Party. It also analyses the continued Protestant attempts to influence Australian life which emphasised moral reform much more than social justice. The chapter concludes with an analysis of why Aborigines had no place in the Protestant vision of a Christian nation.

Churches and industrial disorder

The conservative nature of the Christian churches was clearly indicated in their general reaction to a rash of strikes, commencing with an Australia-wide shipping and seaport strike in 1890. There was some sympathy for the strikers in non-labour circles. They received support from Chief Justice Higinbotham in Victoria and the radically inclined Chief Justice of Queensland, Charles Lilley, who never exhibited any deep religious convictions. Australia's leading Roman Catholic prelate, Cardinal Patrick Moran, the Archbishop of Sydney, also supported publicly in 1890 the aims of the maritime strike. However, after his offer of mediation was opposed by employers, he shunned further publicity on the issue. Melbourne's Catholic Archbishop Thomas Carr, who supported housing for the poor, education for women and child endowment, vainly advocated conferences between workers and employers. But Carr and other Australian bishops were careful not to express public approval of the strikers' aims.

Among Protestants there was less sympathy for the plight of the generally underpaid striking workers. Melbourne's Anglican archbishop, Dr Field Goe, described the unions' at times strong arm attempts to stop the breaking of strikes with non union labour as 'sheer tyranny'.[1] In Brisbane, the Anglican Bishop William Webber's proclamation of a neutral stance was compromised by his support for freedom of contract for non-union workers. Most of the Protestant clergy refused to take sides, and their church councils passed vapid resolutions calling for conciliation. One of the very few Protestant clergy trusted by Queensland workers was the eminent Baptist W. Whale, who in 1895 arbitrated successfully a bitter strike by bootmakers. The unionists' new newspaper, the Brisbane *Worker*, claimed rightly that most nonconformist ministers had 'either rounded on the strikers or carefully straddled the fence'.[2]

In South Australia, among the small Primitive Methodist denomination, there was some sympathy for the aspirations of workers. The Rev. Hugh Gilmore in 1890 publicly supported striking dockers in Port Adelaide and recommended State ownership of the shipping industry. Also, a Wesleyan Methodist minister in Adelaide, Joseph Berry, supported the right of unionists to strike. However, when in 1892 four young ministers during the South Australian Wesleyan Conference called publicly for an 'enquiry into the condition of the working classes', their action was disowned by the conference.[3]

In Sydney the main response of clergy who commented on the strike was in line with Wesleyan minister Rainsford Bavin, who suggested that ship captains and their crew should pray together. There was an attempt by Congregationalist minister Dr Thomas Roseby and some other liberal-minded Protestant clergy to offer conciliation, which was rejected by employers bent on unconditional unionist surrender. The Sydney Labour Defence Committee condemned the clergy for leaving public opinion 'to grope amid the gloom of *sacerdotal* clap trap' except for a few, such as Roseby and Moran, who displayed 'Christ-like sympathy for the struggling masses'.[4]

Christian responses to economic depression

It is true that many clergy had become disturbed about the savage depression which had burst the bubble of 1880s prosperity in Australia. However, the prevalent Protestant view was to claim that the depressed times were a symptom of spiritual decline and that the cure was winning individual souls to Christ and uplifting the moral tone of society. The 1892 Sydney Wesleyan Methodist Conference's sanctimonious reaction was: 'Have not commercial disasters, sickness and death followed because sin preceded'?[5] The inner-Melbourne Wesleyan evangelist Henry Hall agreed that the depression was God's judgment on sinful people and had no opinion about the need for economic reform. The only change in his response to the poor caused by the depression was to give handouts to the poor, which previously he had avoided so as not to create slothfulness.

Indeed, responses by the churches to the additional poverty created by the depression were in terms of traditional charity. In this age of no government dole, churches were a vital link between the better off and the much greater numbers of unemployed and other economically destitute victims of the depression. In the Anglican Sydney diocese, the new order of deaconesses was an additional source of assistance in delivering food and clothing to destitute families. In the Presbyterian Church in Victoria Dorcas Societies, with heavy female involvement, devoted time to visiting the sick and delivering goods to the poor. In South Australia, charitable activities went a step further with the Wesleyan Conference urging the government to spend money on public works to give work to the unemployed and the church supporting a village settlement scheme along the Murray River. Some Methodist ministers were calling for the development of a social welfare state, but they were a small minority.

In the Catholic Church the new St Vincent de Paul Society became a major agency for giving assistance to needy families. But it had the same approach of rescuing fallen individuals and had no thoughts about the need to change the social order, believing that its social work was the means of dissolving class tensions and that economic inequality was preordained to allow the glorious work of charity. Its president from 1895 to 1917, Louis Hedon, a lawyer and non-Labor member of the New South Wales Legislative Council, reflected on the 1890s era of strikes and depression, by writing in his 1902 Society report: 'Society could not be dissolved and class would never war against class while such exercises of charity existed. Providence would give the poor the gift of patience and would give the wealthy the gift of sympathy and practical benevolence'.[6]

Churches and politics

Protestant churches also did not give much support to the emerging Labor Party. Only a small handful of Sydney clergymen, such as Roseby and a Presbyterian minister, James Milne, expressed any public approval of the party. However, there were a significant number of practising Protestants in the early ranks of the New South Wales party, such as Methodist lay preachers Alfred Edden, Francis Cotton, John Fegan and George Clark and Anglican Sunday-School superintendent James McGowen. The prominence of Methodists reflected the working class people in their ranks and the involvement of Methodists in trade unions and early Labour Party politics in Britain. These Protestants produced an early pro-temperance reform block in the party. The Catholic *Freeman's Journal* observed in 1896 that 'the Labour [*sic*] Party is largely composed of pulpit-punchers and local preachers'.[7] Evangelical Protestants also have been credited as lending to the party its secular evangelical-style brotherhood fervour.

However, the influence of committed Protestants in the New South Wales Labor Party soon diminished with many objecting to the imposition of a pledge to vote for majority decisions of the parliamentary caucus. Clark responded that unless 'a man can hand over to a caucus his religious convictions, his temperance principles, and his freedom of action on moral questions... he has no right... to offer himself as a labour candidate'.[8] Other prominent members of the Party had rejected previous allegiance to churches because of clerical conservatism. After he became unemployed in 1890, Henry Holland left the Salvation Army for its failure to appreciate the causes of his poverty and underwent a conversion to a 'religion of science' based on evolutionary theory. William Morris Hughes, a former teacher in a British Anglican school, considered that no denomination practised Christ's teaching in the sermon on the mount.

In fact, the Catholic Church was the only Australian denomination providing any official support to the Labor Party. This came from the leading Catholic prelate, Bishop Moran. His sympathy for the Labor Party was in line with his support for unionists in the maritime strike. His main motive was the maintenance of social harmony, which he saw would be threatened by denial of legitimate workers' rights. Hence, he welcomed the emergence of a political party 'to protect the working man and to defend his rights in a constitutional manner'.[9] It was not partisan support at this stage. He did not view the Labor Party as promoting any of his major interests, which centered on the growth and cohesion of the Catholic Church in Australia, except perhaps on the education issue. So he did not issue any exhortation to Catholics to vote Labor.

Moran's fellow Australian bishops were less willing to express any public approval of the Labor Party. Carr in Melbourne gave no expression to his private sympathy for the Labor cause. Brisbane's Archbishop, Robert Dunne, alarmed at a socialist threat, damned Labor as a 'plunder and irreligion' party and encouraged Catholics to vote for the largely Protestant government.[10] He was mirroring a general support for capitalism, which encouraged Queensland clergy and many other Australian Catholic priests to oppose the emergence of the Labor Party. This opposition, however, did not stop the movement of Catholic voters to Labor. Moran's public sympathy for the Labor cause was a mere icing on the cake of ready identification between the majority of Catholics who were working class with a party dedicated to further workers' interests.

Indeed, Protestant Christians in the 1890s gave much more support to non-Labor parties. In New South Wales, anti-alcohol advocates, though initially enthused by the early temperance interest in the Labor Party, looked more to the Free Trade Party for support. They were happy when, in the 1894 election, twenty-two of the twenty-six successful metropolitan candidates who signed the temperance pledge were Free Traders. The *Methodist* was pleased to count five Methodists in the new Free Trade ministry. Two others were influential Anglicans, and the Premier, George Reid, was a Presbyterian minister's son and a former secretary of the colony's Young Men's Presbyterian Union. Though he stalled about strengthening earlier local option temperance legislation, his ready reception of church deputations and government action taken in 1897 against Sunday traders kept evangelical Protestants happy.

In South Australia some staunch Methodists, such as Tom Price and John Verran, were Labor politicians. Indeed, the trade union movement in that colony had a significant Methodist leadership, replicating a similar influence in trade unionism in the parts of England where Methodism was strong. It also has been argued that in South Australia, where nonconformists remained a majority into the twentieth century, and where Catholicism was small, the working class was influenced by Protestant values of thrift, loyalty, self-improvement and general 'respectability'. Therefore, workers were disposed to accept the social order and participate in 'proper channels' of class action, with a notable moderation in South Australian unionism.[11]

Also in South Australia in the 1890s there was increasing criticism of the Methodist Church in socialist journals. The church's emphasis on moral reform was seen as precluding interest in wider social reform. The opposition of Wesleyan Methodists, in particular, to socialism was condemned. The fact that the Methodist Church was singled out for criticism indicated its pervasive presence in South Australia. Although committed Methodists remained among the Labor leadership, they were a distinct minority. Only seven of 54 labour leaders, who featured in 'Our Roll of Honour' in the *Weekly Herald* during 1896 and 1897, were active Methodists.[12]

In fact most prominent Methodists who were involved in South Australian politics, such as Alfred Catt, John Carr, Theodore Hack and Frederick Holder, belonged to non-Labor parties. Many of the senior conservative South Australian politicians were Anglicans, like Richard Chaffey Baker and John Downer. In Victoria influential Presbyterians, such as James Balfour, Robert Harper, James McBain and James Munro were prominent members of the Victorian political establishment.

Furthermore, some pillars of Protestant society in Victoria were revealed, with the impact of the 1890s depression, to have had bases of crumbling financial clay. Munro, a member of the Board of the Management of Toorak Presbyterian Church and prominent in temperance movements, was one of the financiers whose extravagance and recklessness in land speculation had contributed to the especial savagery of the depression in Victoria. When his financial empire started to collapse, he presided, as the Premier of Victoria, over the rushing through Parliament of the *Voluntary Liquidation Act* in December 1891. This legislation prevented depositors in banks and building societies and minority shareholders of companies from forcing a business into liquidation if it could not pay on demand. Munro's justification was to avert any public financial panic. However, he was one of the first to use this Act by suspending payments of two building societies in which he held controlling interests, and then he escaped immediate public retribution by resigning as Premier and arranging his appointment as Victoria's Agent General in London. At least he soon returned to face bankruptcy, unlike other financiers who secretly made deals with creditors to pay minute proportions of their debts and thus escape public ignominy, including Munro's son, John, a Presbyterian elder. James Munro had to give up his suburban Armadale mansion, which ironically later became the Melbourne Bible Institute, and was ordered not to be released from bankruptcy until he repaid seven shillings in the pound. He ended up paying nothing. In all, he lost £608 000 on his land deals, while many investors in his companies were ruined, including one burly labourer who in 1893 delivered him a knock-out punch in a Melbourne street.

It is true that some Protestants supported reforms in the interests of the working class. In Victoria, some liberal minded clergy were prominent in an agitation for factory legislation, which led to the foundation of an anti-sweating league in 1895. Wesleyan minister, Alexander Edgar, preached against the exploitation or 'sweating' of labour, and his Wesley Church in Melbourne was used for Sunday meetings on the issue. Leading light in the Anti-Sweating League, Samuel Mauger, was a Congregationalist Sunday School teacher, temperance advocate and early Labor supporter, who refused to join the Party because of the caucus pledge. He was one of the architects of the resultant 1896 Victorian *Factories Act*. However, its success belonged to a coalition that was much broader than church activists. It included trade unionists, secular liberals and the Melbourne *Age*, whose politically influential owner, David Syme, had abandoned the Presbyterian Church, though it has been argued that he was deeply influenced by his Scottish Calvinist upbringing.[13]

Another reform program supported by many male Protestants was women's suffrage. This was backed by liberals to overcome a form of discrimination and by evangelicals desiring to recruit women voters who were likely to support temperance and other moral reforms. The support of conservative Protestants for women's suffrage was a factor in the easy achievement of this reform in Australia compared with Great Britain.

Women were also prominent in the pressure for women's suffrage in all Australian States, especially those belonging to the Women's Christian Temperance Union (WCTU). An import from the United

States in 1882, this interdenominational Protestant movement grew rapidly in the early 1890s as another Christian reaction to the trauma of the times. Its membership of 7400 in 1894 was as great, in proportion to the total population, as its influential American mother. While the WCTU was not the first temperance body in Australia to involve women, it was the first to be organised by and for women and to be involved in political agitation. As well as temperance, the WCTU was concerned with a great range of other concerns, such as women's suffrage, prostitution, gambling and sabbatarianism. The movement gave women experience in public speaking, organisation of meetings, lobbying politicians, and publishing literature. It also gave them a sense of sisterhood with American and wider world colleagues and provided a base for challenging male domination of society. However, these women were middle class. A study of the WCTU in Victoria suggests that they were mainly wives of self-employed commercial and professional men.[14] WCTU reforms and other progressive Protestant social programs were essentially advanced in the interests of the liberal ideal of equality of opportunity rather than representing any bias towards the interests of the working class.

Only a very small minority of Australian clergy supported socialism. The journal of the small Christian Socialistic Association in Melbourne condemned the churches in 1890 for fostering the viewpoint of most socialists that religious belief was opposed to social reform. Indeed, Christians embracing socialism had difficulty in remaining within mainline churches. An example was Archibald Turnbull, an Anglican priest, who campaigned in Hobart on behalf of the unemployed. For this and other more personal reasons he fell out of favour with Bishop Montgomery, who admitted that his main interests did not embrace social reform. Defrocked for deliberately flouting Montgomery's authority, Turnbull moved in 1896 to Melbourne to found the Labour Church, which developed close relations with the Victorian Socialists' League and with the Trades Hall Council. His funeral in 1901 was conducted by Charles Strong, who had come to believe that socialism was complementary with Christianity. His Australian Church was a worshipping home for Alice Henry, a leading campaigner in Victoria for women's suffrage and advocate for female involvement in the union movement. She was attracted by Strong's liberal preaching and discussions in his church of issues such as 'the Woman Question' in her spiritual journey from puritanical Presbyterianism to Fabian socialism.[15]

However, among socialists and the wider working class there was significant secularist opposition to Christianity. Socialist leaders tended to be aggressively atheist, especially those influenced by Marxist ideology and the anti-clericalism of socialism in continental Europe. Socialism was a major counter influence to Methodism and Catholicism in the trade union movement, though its impact was very diverse. It gave to workers a non-religious confidence in the future. However, the non-deliverance of 'Socialism in Our Time', the failure of socialist cooperative movements and the inability to implement relevant political reforms were reasons for the downturn in socialism's influence in the early twentieth century. But, within the pragmatic 'labourism' which became predominant, there was a strong secularist influence which influenced Labor Parties to reject firmly state aid for Catholic schools.

Some anti-establishment journalists were leaders of anti-clerical secularism. The widely-circulating *Bulletin* was an apostle of anti-clericalism in Australia with its cartoons representing black frock-coated, umbrella carrying and finger-waving parsons attempting to impose puritanical values on disdainful workers. Other journalists responded to Protestant wowserism and to the allure of handsome profits by publishing salacious hedonism, exemplified by John Norton, the hard-drinking owner and editor from 1896 of the Sydney *Truth*. His scandalous and risque material enjoyed sky-rocketing sales. He established local editions of *Truth* in Queensland, Western Australia and Victoria, from where South Australian and Tasmanian editions were printed. He is credited with a wide influence on popular attitudes, which included exposés of capitalist abuses and trumpeting of White Australian racism. However, Norton also retained sincerely-held private religious beliefs, and his marriage and funeral were in Anglican churches.

Churches and Australian federation

Federation was an opportunity for the Protestant churches to assert their conviction that the new Australian Commonwealth would be a Christian nation. At the People's Convention in Bathurst, New South Wales, a Congregationalist liberal theologian from Victoria, Alexander Gosman, moved that by acknowledging 'the existence of a widespread belief in the government of the world by Divine Providence, ... the Supreme Ruler may be invoked to further, if it please Him, the Federal Movement'. The motion aroused a storm of criticism from other delegates who objected to raising religious issues, though usually affirming their own belief in God. Gosman withdrew his motion, but on the last day of the convention, when many were absent, a compromise resolution, 'acknowledging the Government of the World by Divine Providence', was passed.[16]

This resolution did not guarantee that God would be recognised in the new constitution. Seventh Day Adventists, recent arrivals from the United States and fearing a replication in the Australian Commonwealth of American pressure for federal Sunday laws, fiercely argued the cause of complete separation of church and state. Even though the Adventists were a miniscule 0.09% of the Australian population in 1901, their arguments echoed former dissenting orthodoxy in the age of Anglican supremacy and struck enough resonance for God to be omitted at the federal convention meeting in Adelaide in 1897. They received valuable support from Edmund Barton, an eminent lawyer who was an Anglican Freemason. He declared that the business of a secular state, 'however deeply Christian, unless it has an established church, unless religion is interwoven expressly and professedly with all its actions' must be 'distinguished from religious business'.[17]

However, times had changed in the late 1890s from the dissenting past. Protestant clergy had a new concern to demonstrate that Australia was genuinely a Christian nation. Their confidence in this reality had been dented by the traumas of the depression of the 1890s; the diminishing status of clergy in the community; the strength of the opposition to sabbatarian and temperance ideals, and by the new secularist challenges to Christianity. They were clinging to a vision of transforming Australia into a holy nation, which had energised their campaigns for moral reforms.

So an intense agitation was launched by Protestant councils of churches, which had been established to meet such challenges, and by many clergy to restore God to the constitution. They enlisted in the process the support of all but the Tasmanian colonial parliaments. A Catholic, a cultured Adelaide barrister, Patrick McMahon Glynn, was recruited to move the restoration of God at the next convention in Melbourne. Glynn succeeded in a climate in which most delegates saw the clear drift of public opinion and approved a preamble in which the Australian people, 'humbly relying on the blessing of Almighty God', agreed to unite in a Federal Commonwealth. But a leader of the separatist cause, Henry Bournes

Higgins, an intellectual lawyer who had rejected the institutional church though retaining an inner spirituality, succeeded in enshrining a clause in the constitution which forbad the Commonwealth from establishing any religion, from imposing religious observations or tests, or from prohibiting 'the free exercise of any religion'. This clause expressed the reality of separation of church and state in late nineteenth-century Australia, and was welcomed by some, but not all, Protestants.

The result of the debate over the inclusion of God in the Australian constitution demonstrated that the big majority of Australians still believed in the Christian deity. The proportion of the 3.78 million non-Aboriginal Australians denying or refusing in 1901 to state any religion was only 1.9%, and 96.2% said they were Christians. This was an actual increase of 1% since 1891, which reflected a small decline in the non-religious category and a drop in the Chinese Buddhist population.[18] The public face of Australia was still firmly Christian. Almost all marriages were conducted in Christian churches. Only a few parents dared to leave their children unbaptised. Churches were the location of nearly all funerals. Public morality was firmly based on Protestant Christian principles.

Private practice of the faith always had been less than this public display of Christianity. Nevertheless, during the more uncertain 1890s church attendances had further increased. The official 49% of the population of Victoria attending Church services each Sunday was probably inflated — it would have been 74% of the 'adult' population over fourteen years of age. In New South Wales regular church attendances had risen by one percentage point to 28% of the total population or 45% of the 'adults'.[19]

Protestant moral reform

The big gap between public faith and private practice in New South Wales made many Protestant Christians there anxious for the future. They had celebrated their victory over the incorporation of God in the constitution and the inauguration of the Australian nation on 1 January 1901 with great enthusiasm. But there was a realisation that much effort was needed to overcome the religious indifference and perceived moral laxity in the new nation, as expressed by a militant champion of the Sydney Protestant cause, the Rev. William M. Dill Macky to the New South Wales Presbyterian Assembly: 'Sabbath desecration — impurity and vice seem to me to be on the increase in spite of all our efforts'.[20]

Much of the consequent Protestant effort to 1914 was involved in church growth activities, such as building additional churches, recruiting and educating more clergy, expansion of Sunday schools, and revivalist campaigns assisted by visiting overseas evangelists. A prominent example of these campaigns was the second visit in 1909 of American gospel singer and hymn writer, Charles Alexander, in the company of American evangelist Dr Wilbur Chapman for a five week mission on behalf of the Evangelical Council of New South Wales. Crowds as large as 7000 flocked to hear them. As many as 1500 people made a decision for Christ on one night in the Sydney Town Hall, where meetings outshone concurrent concerts given by the already legendary Australian singer Nellie Melba. Perhaps 10 000 people made new decisions for Christ during the campaign, and in 1909 the Methodist Church received 2000 new members, three times the normal increase. But most of those who attended the meetings were established church goers. Though there was a flow on of evangelistic activities, especially among Methodists, theirs and other Protestant churches were more revitalised than enlarged. Special efforts to reach the working classes, such as the Anglican declaration of inner Sydney as a mission zone, largely failed. The Protestant churches remained basically middle class with the addition of some skilled workers. However, one exception had been the success in the Illawarra mining region, where a tent mission revival had added 2753 new converts, especially to the newly united Methodist church, which equalled 15% of the region's population.[21] Indeed, the gain in membership of New South Wales Methodist churches from 1901 to 1911 was a good 56% — the largest of any of the main-line Protestant denominations. By contrast, the number not stating any religion rose in that decade by over two-thirds, even though they were only 2.3% of the State's population.[22]

The Protestants continued their campaign for moral reform in the years from 1900 to the First World War. It has been argued by J.D. Bollen that in New South Wales social justice reform was also prominent. He points to the influence of social gospel thought from Britain that received a receptive ear among Australian Protestants as a result of the traumas of the depression and strikes of the early 1890s. He cities as an example the decision by the 1898 Anglican Archbishop's conference in Sydney to form the Christian Social Union to study how 'moral truths and the principles of Christianity' could be applied 'to the social and economic difficulties of the present time' and 'to present Christ in practical life'.[23] But its membership was neither large nor influential and it was short-lived. Bollen can only point to clerical and lay expressions of concern on issues of human welfare, such as minimum wages and old age pensions, and a welcoming of the Carruthers and Wade Liberal New South Wales Governments of 1904–10 for enacting such measures.

There is a contrary argument that moral reform was pre-eminent in the minds and community activities of Australian Protestants. A good case was Methodism in South Australia, which was united as one body in 1900 and which was easily the largest non-Anglican Protestant denomination in that State. In Methodist tradition there were strands of social justice concern in the English homeland. A prominent example in England was the Forward Movement of the 1880s, a largely Methodist organisation emphasising social concern for the victims of urban society. This movement was led by Wesleyan minister Hugh Price Hughes, a Christian Socialist, who supported state intervention to regenerate society and inveighed against the exploiting rich. One of his oft repeated phrases, the 'Nonconformist Conscience', was used by some South Australian Methodists around the turn of the century to justify their church's social reform concerns. However, even Hughes placed his highest priority on moral reform of the poor and became a champion in England of the temperance movement. Likewise, moral reform to abolish legalised gambling, to enforce the Sabbatarian Sunday, and especially to impose temperance ideals, were the priorities of South Australian Methodism. After the 1900 union, the annual conference constantly resolved 'that the Conference regards intemperance as amongst the most serious moral and social evils now prevalent', and Methodists were urged 'to promote all legislative measures which aim at the restraint or extinction of the liquor traffic'.[24]

Moral reform, argues Richard Broome, was also the priority of Protestants in New South Wales. They pressed for a more strict Sabbath by ending illegal trading and liquor sales on Sundays; the strengthening of local option to ban the sale of alcohol; stricter sexual purity by regulating dancing halls and prohibiting contraception devices; the banning of newly introduced mixed sea bathing, and the suppression of gambling. Protestant support for the Carruthers–Wade governments was mainly for their willingness to legislate on such issues. The Liberals won the 1904 election principally because of the Protestant and temperance vote, and Carruthers had promised in the campaign to strengthen local option. He duly carried this out with the 1905 *Liquor Act*. It reduced the proportion of the electorate needed for validation of local option decisions from 50% to 30% and greatly strengthened licensing laws, but ironically it led to the suppression of many small hotels in favour of fewer and larger ones controlled by the big brewery companies. The government also obliged by raiding working class illegal gambling dens and by introducing legislation to widen the bans on gambling, though intense Labor and Catholic opposition stopped the prohibition of lotteries and raffles. The 1907 election became a battleground in New South Wales in which church and temperance groups vigorously supported the government, which was returned with a reduced majority. The *Methodist* considered that the increased Labor vote was caused by a combination of 'Rum, Romanism, Socialism and Gambling'.[25]

Renewed sectarianism

This Protestant identifying of the Roman Catholic Church with the Labor opposition to moral reform was an indication of a revival of sectarian politics in New South Wales. Cardinal Moran had some responsibility for this, especially his speech in Sydney in June 1895 on the 'Reunion of Christendom', which centred on the 'failure of Protestant Missions'. This attack on a Protestant holy cow provoked a large meeting in York Street's Centenary Hall, presided over by the Anglican primate, which heard speeches refuting the cardinal's claims. This controversy has been identified as the beginning of the new wave of sectarianism in New South Wales.[26]

However, sectarianism was also exploited by Protestant demagogues. Pre-eminent was Dill Macky, who brought the bitterness of his Northern Irish background to tirades about the threat of Romanism. He was instrumental in founding a Protestant Defence Association in 1903, which quickly claimed 16 000 members. The extremism of his rhetoric was exemplified by his comment that 'if the Roman Catholic Church could again introduce the thumbscrew, the faggot, and the stake, it would do so'.[27] The personal intensity of his crusade was demonstrated by his intervention in a sectarian *cause célèbre* in 1900: a divorce suit by Arthur Coningham, an Anglican former cricketer and discharged bankrupt, who claimed £5000 damages from the alleged co-respondent, Father Denis O'Haran, Moran's confidante and private secretary. Firmly believing in Mrs Alice Coningham's confession of adultery with O'Haran, Dill Macky gave Coningham financial aid and even lent him a revolver. But in the constant uproar over legitimate Catholic cries of a frame-up, Coningham lost the case and fled to New Zealand where he was imprisoned for six months in 1903 for fraudulence and in 1912 was divorced by his wife for adultery.

Another issue emerged at this time which further widened the gap between Catholicism and Protestantism. This was the outbreak of the Boer War in 1899, which involved the first major overseas Australian troop commitment. Protestant Churches generally showed their conservative attachment to British imperialism by vigorously supporting the British cause against Boer independence. The New South Wales Methodist Conference recognised in the war 'the hand of God', and the Anglican Synod of Victoria promised every facility to chaplains to perform their duty for 'God, their Queen, and their country'.[28]

Only a few Protestants expressed opposition to the war. The Rev. Professor John Rentoul, master of the Presbyterian Ormond College at Melbourne University, who at that stage of his life was a pacifist, spoke out fearlessly against the war. But he received very little support from fellow Presbyterians. Another opponent of the war was George Arnold Wood, the theologically trained Congregationalist Professor of History at Sydney University, who from the beginning of the war regarded it as unjust and later protested against the 'infamy' of the incarceration of Boer civilians in British concentration camps. The strong Christian support for this war was probably one of the forces impelling him, reluctantly, along the road to agnosticism. Another Christian opponent of the war was Charles Strong, a convinced pacifist, who carried out a vehement campaign against the war and British imperialism, earning him significant unpopularity.

Catholics were much more divided in their response to the Boer War. Some of the 16000 troops sent to South Africa were Catholics, and there was enthusiasm for the imperialist cause in some quarters, such as the premier Jesuit boys' school, Xavier College, in Melbourne. However, Cardinal Moran was sympathetic to the Boer cause and considered that Australians should not be involved in suppressing it. He and other Irish clergy tended to identify that cause with the struggle for Irish independence from British rule. A consequence was Protestant suspicion of Catholic loyalty. A Catholic chaplain in the second Australian contingent to South Africa was provoked to respond in January 1900 that one of his motives for enlisting was a desire 'that by his action he should give denial to the calumny put forward by the press regarding the attitude of the Irish in Australia'.[29]

The growing separation of the Protestant and Catholic communities in Australia encouraged sectarian rivalry. The independent Catholic school system, which was increasingly incorporating Catholic children, was producing early-age religious rivalry demonstrated by jibes and at times sticks and stones hurled between Catholic and state school children. The increasing size and industrialisation of the big cities had witnessed a flight of the largely Protestant middle class to mushrooming suburbs and a congregation of the significantly Catholic working class in crowded and squalid inner city tenements. Consolidation of rural properties with the harsh vagaries of the Australian climate was pressing poorer small farmers, many of whom were Catholics, into the inner urban unskilled work force. The Protestant moral campaigns against drinking and gambling and liberalisation of Sundays were blows at some of the few pleasures of working class lives. The strikes of the early 1890s increased Protestant criticisms of working class attitudes, and the caucus pledge in the Labor Party had driven many church-attending Protestants from its ranks. The identification of New South Wales Protestants with the Free Trade and Liberal Parties increased the Catholic identification with Labor, exemplified by Cardinal Moran's comment in 1903 that Labor was 'the only party above religious prejudice'.[30]

Catholicism and the Labor Party

However, the Catholic impact on the Labor Party was conservative. Catholicism was one of the influences within the Party that resulted in the defeat of committed socialists to control it. This attempt reached a high point in 1896 when the New South Wales' Party adopted a general platform committed to the nationalisation of land and the means of production, distribution and exchange. But this commitment never became part of the Party's fighting platform, and after 1896 the influence of socialists declined.

Campaigns by Cardinal Moran and other Catholic leaders against socialism were one reason for its decline. In 1897, Moran stood for a seat at the Federal Convention in order to stop the election in New

South Wales of any socialist Labor delegate. This strategy worked as, although unsuccessful, his standing split the Labor vote. Fearing continued socialist influence within the Party, a lay Catholic member, H.E. Kelly, publicly condemned the endorsement by a 1905 Political Labour Leagues conference in Sydney of a general principle in favour of 'the securing of the full results of their industry to all producers by the collective ownership of monopolies and the extension of the industrial and economic functions of the State and municipality'. Kelly argued that this statement was in conflict with Pope Leo XIII's condemnation of socialism in his 1891 encyclical, *Rerum Novarum*, and pointed out that 90% of Catholics had voted Labor in 1904. It is probable, however, that his objection had been taken into account in the watering down of the original motion at the conference to 'a Cooperative Commonwealth founded on the socialisation of the production and distribution of wealth'.[31] Cardinal Moran was happy to accept this definition, believing that the Labor Party in Australia had none of the violence and atheism of European socialism.

But in no sense did the Catholic Church have a controlling interest in Australian Labor Parties. Others also opposed socialism such as pragmatists concerned to broaden the party's electoral appeal, especially the powerful Australian Workers' Union (AWU), which did not have many Catholics in its leadership and which was interested in practical reforms. One of the Protestant anti-socialists, the Party's leader from 1894 to 1913, James McGowen, may also have been influenced by his active involvement at St Paul's Anglican Church at Redfern. In the New South Wales Labor Party, Catholics were never a majority among its parliamentary members before 1914, though their proportion did increase from a mere 8% in 1891 to 39% in 1910.[32] The Party leadership to 1916 was non-Catholic: McGowen and William Holman, who was nominally Anglican. Holman, the New South Wales Labor Premier from 1913 to 1916 believed in home rule for Ireland and was generally sympathetic to the Catholic Church. However, when in the 1913 State election campaign the Catholic Federation of New South Wales asked all Labor candidates to promise to support state aid for Catholic schools and hospitals, Holman reminded Party members that they could not give any pledge to a non-party organisation. He knew that his Party depended on many more than the 25% of the State's population who were Catholic in 1911.

In Victoria, where Catholics were 22% of the 1911 population, their church leaders were less enthusiastic about the Labor Party than in

New South Wales. Sectarianism had not existed to the same extent in Victoria. One reason for this was the way evangelicals had maintained their grip on sabbatarian Sundays. Tighter licensing laws restricted the sale of alcohol in Victoria to hotels and designated wine shops, and later, in the 1920s, there were local option victories in imposing prohibition in a band of Melbourne's middle class eastern suburbs from Camberwell to Box Hill. These successes, and the larger proportion of church-attenders in Victoria, encouraged less of a siege mentality among Protestant clergy in Melbourne than in Sydney. The evangelically influenced gold-migrant generation had created an easier alliance between church and establishment in Victoria than in New South Wales, with its shallower religious roots. There was also a broader church and more liberal influence in Melbourne's Protestant denominations, especially in the Church of England, which narrowed the area of potential support for the Dill Macky brand of sectarianism.

Nor was there the same extent of political exploitation of religious rivalry in Victorian politics. Influential Victorian liberal Protestants, such as Samuel Mauger and Hume Cook in federal politics, represented electorates with large working class constituencies, making it unwise for them to join a sectarian crusade. The Labor Party in Victoria also gave support to temperance reform. Influential was medical doctor William Maloney who, although agnostic and married in the Melbourne Registrar's Office, insisted on Catholic baptism for his two children. He considered drunkenness a blight on the employment of and money saving prospects of working men. The temperance ideal had broad acceptance within the Party and was expressed in a policy of nationalisation of the alcohol industry to remove the profit motive for encouraging excessive drinking. The Victorian Labor Party was also committed staunchly to the ideal of secular education. Consequently, though Archbishop Carr sympathised with other social justice aims of the Party, he refused to give it his public support. By the time of the arrival of the nationalist Irish Daniel Mannix as his coadjutor bishop in 1913, Carr was thoroughly disillusioned with the Labor Party.

Limitations to Protestant moral order

The Protestant identification with non-labour parties, however, had not created the desired results of a new moral order. In New South

Wales, the Carruthers–Wade Government's modest achievements on liquor reform were the peak of Protestant political influence. In the 1910 election Labor came to power. Furthermore, the emphasis on moral reform had alienated many citizens. Sabbatarianism ran counter to growing popular Sunday entertainments. The campaign against mixed beach bathing was especially damaging because of the growing popularity of swimming and surfing. The movements against alcohol in New South Wales and other Australian States had not reduced the beer consumption, which rose in Australia from 11.1 gallons per head in 1907 to 13.5 gallons in 1913.[33] The campaign against birth control was not supported by liberal Methodists, but had the strong support of the Catholic Church. It argued that it was necessary to prevent birth control in order to stop an alarming fall in the birth rate. However, the campaign did not have any observable influence on the small rises in Australian birth rates after the dramatic fall of the 1890s, which was the result of improving economic conditions.

Nevertheless, there were still substantial church-influenced controls on Australian behaviour with restrictions on the use of Sundays, extending from bans on trading in Sydney, to the closing of many entertainments and hotels in Melbourne and Adelaide. In Sydney, the mixed bathers were required to wear neck to knee costumes. In the interests of sexual purity, there was also widespread censorship of what Australians could read or watch on the new silent movie screens.

Furthermore, despite the nominal nature of the religious practice of many Australian Protestants, the leading church spokesmen still had community authority. Their sermons were regularly printed at length in newspapers. Their views on moral issues carried weight. Some even achieved high public prominence. William Fitchett, a leading Methodist minister in Melbourne, was the author of *Deeds that Won the Empire*, first published in 1897 and selling over 250000 copies across the British empire. Such imperial zeal had been commonly expressed by Protestant clergy since the Boer War and was to be a feature of their reaction to the next war.

Social Darwinism, paternalism and Aborigines

Aboriginal people were not part of the Protestant vision for a Christian Australia. In the late nineteenth century there was a common view that Aborigines were an inferior people and a dying race, and that this was a natural course of events. It has been claimed that such prejudice about indigenous Australians was influenced by the impact of social Darwinism: a translation of Darwin's theory of natural selection and the survival of the fittest from the physical world to human society. In this way Darwinism gave a pseudo-scientific support to the racism which already infected white Australian views of Aborigines. Social Darwinism enhanced the viewpoint that Aborigines were at the bottom of the social scale, as demonstrated by their perceived nomadic society, compared with agriculturally-based Pacific Islanders. The decline of the Australian Aboriginal population with the violence and diseases introduced by white invaders, was a further demonstration that they were destined to disappear in the struggle for the survival of the fittest race.

The influence of Darwinian ideas, however, was more complex than merely the enhancement and legitimation of racism. People who already believed in the inferiority of Aborigines certainly used these ideas to justify ignoring Aboriginal rights in the exploitation of their land. However, studies of the impact of Darwinian thought in the United States, as transmitted by Herbert Spencer and his American disciples, suggest that it also encouraged a paternalistic attitude towards African-Americans expressed in philanthropic programs.[34]

Paternalism, certainly, was the main contribution of Darwinism to the 'Aboriginal problem' as conceived by Australian missionaries and other Christians. Even John Gribble, one of the most aggressive defenders of Aboriginal rights, believed in the innate inferiority of and likely extinction of indigenous Australians. Yarrabah Mission in northern Queensland, which he founded in 1892 after his confrontations in Western Australia, and which was continued after his death in 1893 by his son Ernest Gribble, was a paternalistic institution. Ernest, like his father before him, believed it his duty to save 'the remnant that is left' of the vanishing Aboriginal race. He sought to segregate his charges from 'degrading' European and Chinese influences, and restore Aborigines' self-respect through Christian teaching and inculcation of the work ethic. In this cause, young children were separated from their parents and given English language education and Christian indoctrination. The mission would become 'a permanent home for the blacks'.[35] At least, though having a low opinion of Aboriginal culture, he allowed indigenous ceremonies to continue in the belief that they would gradually die out. He also permitted Aborigines to hunt for their food in the traditional manner and was pleased to discover before he left Yarrabah in 1913 that births at the mission exceeded deaths. But he strictly controlled the lives of the mission people, and he approved the segregationist provisions of the 1897 Queensland *Aborigines Protection and the Sale of Opium Act*.

This Queensland legislation grew from an era when virtual open-season killing of Aborigines had been sanctioned. The conflict was exacerbated by the strong Aboriginal resistance against the white invasion of Australia in a region of high Aboriginal population and within a favourable environment of forests and mountains for guerilla warfare. In this tropical coastal region of Queensland, over 300 Europeans were killed by Aborigines from 1860 to 1900. Despite this resistance, by the 1890s the original Aboriginal population in Queensland of over 100 000 had been reduced to a mere 15 000. The Christian churches had paid little attention to this unfolding disaster, but in 1891, the Victorian Presbyterian Church finally took action to establish the Mapoon mission on the Gulf coast of Cape York. The pioneer of this mission, James Ward, said that Presbyterian authorities in Queensland considered that 'men who were going to devote their lives to such despicable work are expected to be ne'er-do-wells'.[36] The Queensland Anglican Church's neglect of Aboriginal missions forced Gribble to pay his own expenses in establishing Yarrabah.

It was left to an Anglican politician, Horace Tozer, and a Scottish-born public servant of no known religious persuasion, Archibald Meston, who as a child in northern New South Wales had learned an Aboriginal language, to introduce reforming legislation. The 1897 *Protection Act* was based on Meston's report of an investigation into the condition of Queensland's Aborigines, commissioned in 1894. Tozer hoped to regain 'freedom of life and action' for Aborigines by establishing reserves they could enter by choice. But Meston paid no recognition to the bond between Aborigines and their own land. He insisted that, 'for their own benefit', they must be confined to the five large self-sufficient and ten smaller reserves established by the Act.[37] Government authorities had the power to prohibit anybody from entering a reserve and controlled the movements, wages and even the marriage rights of the Aborigines living there. 'Troublesome' people could be transferred to more distant settlements; families could be forcibly split. The education policies of the reserves reflected the paternalistic control. The chief protector from 1904–1906, Walter Roth, who as an anthropologist had studied and published on Aboriginal culture, considered that 'no practically useful results can possibly accrue from teaching our mainland blacks composition, fractions, decimals and any other subjects that will in any way enable them to come into competition with Europeans'.[38] Queensland's Aborigines were to live under government-controlled segregation, except where their unskilled labour could be utilised. A similar pattern, with variations, was established in the other States, except Tasmania, where there were only a few survivors of the indigenous race.

The anthropological studies of Roth and others from the 1870s did assist Christian missionaries and some other Australians to change their previous complete contempt for Aboriginal culture. However, in this anthropological research, social Darwinism reinforced the view that the Aborigines, though a distinctive and interesting race, were the most culturally backward people in the world. The research also started the process of removal of Aboriginal artifacts, including bones from sacred burial sites, to city museums, which showed a complete disregard for Aboriginal sensitivities and religion.

The new anthropological knowledge did make some missionaries interfere less with Aboriginal practices. There was also some change in the previous attitude of early missionaries that Aborigines had no religious beliefs at all. However, most missionaries regarded Aboriginal religious beliefs as evil or having no intrinsic worth. Rarer was the Victorian Anglican missionary John Bulmer's admission that Aboriginal myths might be on a par with Greek mythology. Unparalleled in the nineteenth century, was the opinion of the well-educated Presbyterian missionary, William Ridley, who worked among Aborigines in the Moreton Bay and Darling Downs districts in Queensland in the mid-1850s. He recognised that Aboriginal spirituality was 'the thirst for religious mystery', a reaching out to God.[39] However, for all nineteenth-century missionaries, the new knowledge about Aboriginal customs and religion did not upset their paternalistic notions of the superiority of British culture, which they expected to prevail.

Summary

Through the depression of the 1890s and the early years of the new Commonwealth Protestants demonstrated their conservative influence on Australian life. Few clergy had been willing to side with the industrial and political aspirations of workers and had identified much more closely with non-Labor political parties. While some clergy and lay Protestants supported new social gospel ideas, the main Protestant emphasis was on moral, especially temperance reform, in a drive to maintain a Christian nation in which the allegedly declining Aboriginal race had no future place. However, one of the by-products of Protestant moral reform was support for women's suffrage and the provision of an avenue for female activism. By 1914 there was little progress in the temperance movement, a decline of sabbatarianism, and even a failure to block the spread of birth control, though other sexual puritanism was maintained. Catholics identified more with the Labor Party, where they had an anti-socialist influence; but the leadership of the Party remained non-Catholic, and its support for secular education limited Catholic clergy support.

Chapter Four

Christian Conservatism, *1914–1939*

The outbreak of the First World War saw a renewed identification of Protestant Churches with Australian imperial loyalty. During and after the war there were new outbursts of sectarianism with imputations of Catholic disloyalty in bitter struggles over military conscription, which reinforced separatism between Catholics and Protestants and increased the Catholic identity with the Labor Party. The 1930s were the era of the Great Depression, to which the Church, though not all its members, responded with traditional conservatism. The inter-war years also saw a continuation of paternalistic protection of Aborigines on mission stations, and general church neglect of the exploitation of Aborigines by white society. In this era, there was a further decline in the Protestant moral order and in popular attachment to Protestant, but not to Catholic churches.

Churches and the outbreak of war

The general Protestant response to the outbreak of the First World War in August 1914 was an enthusiastic rally to imperial Britain's side. A constant pulpit refrain was that Australians must do their duty to assist Britain in this noble cause, with much emphasis on Germany's violation of neutral Belgium. There also was a common feeling that out of the evil of war might come the good of Christian revival in Australia, which would fill the gaps of flagging personal faith. John Walker, a prominent Presbyterian minister in Ballarat Victoria, envisaged that the legacy of the war would be a 'fire-purged civilisation, ... [in] which the Cross [would] be the inspiring symbol among all classes of a higher and holier civilisation'.[1] Another strand in the pro-war rhetoric of Protestant churches was opposition to the German Lutheran theology which identified God with German militarism, as expressed by Anglican Canon David Garland in Brisbane. He declared: 'There is not the slightest hope of coming to terms with Prussianism short of absolute surrender'.[2]

Furthermore, Catholic clergy saw the war as an opportunity to demonstrate their national loyalty. Archbishop Michael Kelly in Sydney considered it a just war and lent his active support at recruiting meetings. Archbishop Carr in Melbourne urged his people to 'join heartily with fellow citizens in defence of the mother country'.[3] The Catholic press noted that Ireland had rallied enthusiastically in support of the British war effort. Initial support for the war by the Catholic hierarchy assisted major recruitment of Catholics for the Australian forces. However, the proportion of Catholics enlisting in the Australian Imperial Force in 1914 and 1915 was 18.3%, which was lower than the 22.4% of Catholics in the Australian population in 1911.[4] This reflected some lesser enthusiasm for the war in the Catholic community.

The strong initial support for the war by Catholic and Protestant clergy assisted the massive voluntary enlistment in Australia's expeditionary forces to the Middle East and Western Europe. The churches played a valuable role in sanctifying the cause of the war and giving it a high and noble purpose. It was not an exclusive role. The churches' support was part of a general emphasis by community and government leaders on Australia's identification with the British Empire, causing a Labor Prime Minister to assume automatically that Australia was at war with Germany when Britain declared war.

No Catholic leaders, and very few other Christians, expressed pacifist opposition to the war. However, one prominent Christian pacifist was James Gibson, the editor of the *Messenger of the Presbyterian Church of Queensland* in which he argued his abhorrence for war. But the journal ceased publication in 1916 because of poor circulation. He had only one supporter when he attempted vainly to convince the Queensland Presbyterian Assembly to support his pacifist position. Charles Strong repeated his previous opposition to the Boer War. This time he ran into deeper trouble, with some laypeople reacting by leaving his Australian Church. His wife, Janet, was victimised for her opposition to the war by being pressured to relinquish her position of Vice President of the National Council of Women. The one Christian denomination in Australia opposing the war was the small Society of Friends (Quakers). Its members were committed pacifists, as demonstrated by a leading Quaker, Mary Watts, who berated Garland in a Brisbane street for his militaristic attitude.

Garland and other militant clergy also contributed to a xenophobic atmosphere in which the Lutheran churches in Australia were victimised because of their close identity with the population of German descent — significant in South Australia and Queensland. Lutherans in those States in 1911 comprised 7% and 4% of the population respectively. Pastor Theodore Nickel, the South Australian President of the Evangelical Lutheran Synod of Australia, insisted in a letter to Prime Minister Andrew Fisher in December 1914 that his church was Australian, not German, and that Australian Lutherans were 'well aware' of their 'duty towards' the King of the British Empire and the Australian Government.[5] Indeed, Australians with German names were soon being killed by German bullets in Europe. But the close cultural identity between the Lutheran church and German people, with many worship services and school classes using the German language, resulted in Lutheran schools being closed down and others forced to teach only in English. German-born church members, and some Australian-born, were brutally incarcerated in prison camps.

Evangelical Protestants utilised the war to press for more temperance reform. They were inspired by the spirit of self denial accompanying the patriotic fervour, by the argument that drinking opportunities should be restricted for young soldiers, and by the news that King George V had taken a total abstinence pledge for the war's duration. The target was six o'clock closing for hotels in line with the early closing hours which had been introduced for shops earlier in the century. The first success was in South Australia in a referendum in 1915, in which the affirmative vote to close hotels at 6 p.m. was 93000 to 68000. In Sydney, Holman resisted temperance pressure, his party having received financial support from the liquor trade. But some Labor members, led by a Presbyterian elder, Thomas Brown, supported the temperance move. A Liberal win in a by-election, in which the early closing issue figured prominently, convinced Holman to agree to a referendum. The six o'clock option gained 62% of the vote. A similar referendum victory in Tasmania was followed by legislative action in Victoria to close hotels at that time. However, Western Australia and Queensland, where there were Labor governments, did not follow suit. In the other States temperance advocates considered they had achieved a great victory in preventing the night drinking that kept husbands and fathers away from home. But they had introduced the revolting hotel conditions of the six o'clock swill and there was no reduction in the Australian consumption of beer, which slipped during the war but was back to pre-war levels during the 1920s.

Churches and conscription

Two referenda, in October 1916 and December 1917, to endorse the conscription of single men without dependents for war service, produced a revival of sectarian conflict in Australia. It has been thought that Catholic loyalty to the war eroded significantly after the Easter Rebellion in Ireland in 1916, which was savagely suppressed by British troops, and that this was a major reason for the defeat of conscription in both referenda. However, new evidence suggests that this Irish rebellion had little long-term impact on the Australian Catholic community. Catholic army recruits for the war peaked in 1916 at 19.4% of the total, and fell by only 0.6% in the next year.[6]

The working class identity of many Catholics encouraged them to advocate a negative vote in the referendum campaign which had been imposed by the Commonwealth Labor Government over the heads of the majority of Labor Party members. There had been rising disillusionment among workers at the Federal Labor Government's failure to proceed with a promised price control referendum to prevent perceived profiteering by producers and middlemen in an era of inflation caused by shortages of goods and an increase in the money supply. 'I will never give my vote to compulsorily send men from these shores when I see that people are allowed to make extra war profits', explained Thomas Ryan, the new Catholic Premier of Queensland.[7]

In the first referendum campaign, some of the leading opponents of conscription were active Protestants. The leader of the Federal Parliamentary Labor revolt on the issue was Frank Tudor, a Victorian teetotal deacon of the Congregational Church. In South Australia some Methodist Labor politicians, such as Robert Richards, a future leader of the State Party, and Norman Makin, a Methodist local preacher, were strong anti-conscription advocates. While New South Wales, with the largest proportion of Catholic citizens, had the highest percentage of anti-conscription voters, South Australia, with the smallest proportion of Catholics, had the second biggest anti-conscription vote: 57.5%. Significantly, in the three areas of rural South Australia where Methodism was strongest, which were mining districts, the 'no vote' ranged from 72% to 78%.[8]

There was some major Catholic support for conscription. Father Thomas O'Dwyer, rector of Melbourne's Xavier College, who was an Irish member of a family which served the British Empire, advocated conscription as an equal sharing of the necessary burden of the war. There was a tendency for secondary and tertiary educated Catholics to support conscription, and some tried to silence Bishop Mannix, who was the most vociferous Catholic clerical opponent of conscription. When they found this impossible, pressure was placed on other bishops and Catholic clergy to remain silent on the issue, which many did. So a sizeable minority of Catholic voters would have voted 'yes'. Cliometric research into both conscription referenda suggests that, while there was a correlation between anti-conscription voting and regions of Catholic strength, the statistical tendency was no greater than the relationship between working class regions and the 'no' vote. A much greater variable was the propensity for women to vote in favour of conscription, a proportion of whom must have been Catholic.[9]

Nor were all the non-Catholic anti-conscription voters working class. It has been claimed that farmers were a major anti-conscription force. The new cliometric research has suggested that primary producers tended to be pro-conscription at a slightly greater rate than organised labour's tendency against conscription. So the rural vote against conscription could have been more from farm workers and other labourers. Nevertheless, in the non-mining rural areas of South Australia where Methodism was strong, most of these districts recorded a clear majority of 'no' votes. Donald Cameron, the Presbyterian Director of Home Mission in Victoria, discovered the reality of rural Presbyterians opposing conscription, few of whom would have been workers, during his state tours. So he vainly urged his church to adopt impartiality on the issue.

Cameron's failure was an example of the strong support for conscription given by Protestant church leaders. It has been suggested that this involvement in a political issue was 'a new departure for Protestant churchmen'.[10] On the contrary, it was a continuation of their actions since they started using the political system to advance their moral order. In supporting conscription, the churches were also continuing their close involvement with non-Labor political parties, which Prime Minister Hughes and his supporters joined after they were expelled from the Labor Party. It was specious for the editor of Victorian *Presbyterian Messenger* to claim that the 'Presbyterian Church has no politics' when at the same time it urged its readers 'to vote for Mr Hughes and the boys in the trenches'.[11] At the Standing Committee of the South Australian Methodist Conference, the Rev. William Potts had no doubt about the church's right to intervene on the side of the government. He urged his colleagues to campaign actively for a 'yes' vote, reminding them 'that John Wesley, in his day, offered to organise a Battalion of Methodists to help preserve the orderly existence of the State'.[12]

There was a similar situation when Hughes, as Nationalist Party Prime Minister, ordered the other conscription referendum in December 1917 to cope with an alarming decline in recruiting. This time Mannix, who became Archbishop of Melbourne in May 1917, was a more strident campaigner for a 'no vote', and he received much more support from other Catholic bishops. They had seen the way their people had responded in the first campaign, as demonstrated by the huge crowds who came out to cheer Mannix. Protestant leaders redoubled their efforts to support the affirmative cause. But the majority against conscription increased from 72 476 to 166 588.

During the second campaign there were numerous Protestant criticisms of Catholic disloyalty evidenced by alleged diminished Catholic enlistment, which for 1917 was only slightly reduced. The more intense Catholic opposition in the second campaign may have influenced the bigger Catholic decline in enlistments in 1918, but this decline was only 1.6%.[13] This analysis indicates continuing Catholic support for the war, despite increasing opposition by Catholic hierarchy to conscription.

Catholicism and Labor governments in Queensland

A major consequence of the conscription crisis was a closer Catholic identity with the Labor Party. Even in the Queensland party which did not split on this issue, John Adamson, a former Primitive Methodist minister and parliamentary member, resigned because of his concern about growing Catholic influence in the party.

Indeed, the Catholic Church was a significant influence in the Labor governments which ruled Queensland for all but three of the inter-war years. It was not a case of church dominance, more a partnership between church, government and a powerful trade union, the rural-based AWU. Of the three major inter-war Labor Premiers, William McCormack and Edward Theodore were Catholics. The other Premier, William Forgan Smith, was a lapsed Presbyterian, but he maintained good relations with James Duhig, Brisbane's Archbishop from 1917 to 1965. Also seven of Forgan Smith's ten Cabinet members by the mid-1930s were Catholics, a bigger proportion than the 59% of Labor members of Parliament who were Catholic. Furthermore, in the inter-war years, two of the three major State Secretaries of the AWU, William Riordan and Clarence Fallon, were Catholics.

The Catholic influence in the Queensland Labor Party was not strong enough to overcome government opposition to state aid for church schools. But the major presence of Catholics within Labor probably contributed to its transformation from a committed socialist party prior to 1915 to one which rejected anti-capitalist socialism in the 1920s. Also important was the party's need for broad electoral appeal, particularly in its rural heartland, where many of its supporters were sugar farmers and other small property owners. Catholicism, combined with the party's petit-bourgeois support, also encouraged the party's hostility to Communism, which had gained some popularity with the impact of the Bolshevik revolution in Russia. In 1926 the party's two most influential Catholic members, Theodore and McCormack, proposed the anti-Communist pledge for all Labor members, which resulted in the expulsion of prominent militants from the party. There were, of course, other reasons for imposing the pledge, such as the need to hobble the power of the Australian Railways Union, which was not submitting to government and AWU authority.

From Archibishop Duhig's viewpoint, the Catholic Church did well out of the partnership. During the 1930s depression, he was pleased at the amount of relief work done on Catholic Church properties. He was able to make a good financial realisation on one property by influencing the siting of the new Story Street bridge, named after one of his friends. Duhig was comfortable about advising his constituents to vote for the party, knowing that they were a bulwark to future leanings towards socialism. He told a meeting of the Holy

Name Society at Goodna in 1936: 'Go into your Labor organisations and committee meetings and, while you are loyal to your own section of Labor, see that your section does nothing detrimental to your faith'.[14]

Certainly, by 1937 there was a major concern among some Protestants of undue Catholic influence in the Queensland Labor Party. In December 1937, a Protestant Labour Party was launched. Major grievances were preference for Catholics in the public service — the one area of secure jobs — and the fact that Catholic membership in caucus and government far exceeded the 21.8% of Queenslanders who were Catholics in 1933. The new party demanded that Catholics receive no more than their fair share, called for outlawing a recent exemption of churches from local rates, and condemned immigration of Catholic Italians as sugar cane workers in northern Queensland. However, the new party did not succeed in the 1938 election. Though it received more than a third of the votes in two Brisbane electorates, one of which it won, its State-wide performance was only 9% of the total vote. Labor easily retained government. Sectarianism was not a strong enough impulse in Queensland in the late 1930s to change the votes of the majority of the many Protestants who had been supporting Labor.

Catholics and socialism in Tasmania

In Tasmania the Labor Party lost the 1919 election because its Catholic supporters were agitating for state aid for Catholic schools. This pressure had aroused the wrath of the Protestant Loyalist League. Its propaganda accused Irish disloyalists of working to subvert the Labor Party and to undermine Australia's attachment to the British Empire, a legacy of the conscription hatreds that had bitterly divided Tasmania.

Within the Tasmanian Labor Party there was not the same tension between Catholics and socialists as in other States. Catholics comprised 16.6% of the population, a smaller proportion than in the mainland eastern States. However, from 1916 to 1947 the Labor Party's four leaders and Premiers, Joseph Lyons, Albert Ogilvie, Edmund Dwyer-Gray and Robert Cosgrove, were all Catholics. Before the election of the Tasmanian Labor government in 1923 they all described themselves as 'Catholic socialists'. Socialism in the Tasmanian Labor Party was influenced much more by the land nationalisation theories of Henry George than by radical Marxism, befitting Labor's early rural strength among miners and depressed small farmers. Hobart's Archbishop from 1907 to 1926, Patrick Delaney, after a trip to New Zealand in 1907, praised the 'socialism' of the New Zealand Liberal government, and advocated similar attention to the rights of workers and small farmers in Tasmania. Consequently, Catholics in the Tasmanian Labor Party were comfortable about calling themselves socialists.

However, subsequent Tasmanian Labor governments under Catholic leaders showed a lack of commitment to anti-capitalist socialism. Though the party endorsed in 1921 the socialisation of the means of production, distribution and exchange, Lyons was careful to avoid this issue in the 1922 election campaign, and conveniently forgot about the socialist policy when he was Premier. After entering the Federal Parliamentary arena, his economic thinking was so orthodox that he felt impelled to abandon the Federal Labor Party in 1932 and become the first non-Labor Catholic Prime Minister of Australia. The more radical Ogilvie concentrated on a policy of public spending to cope with the impact of the Great Depression of the 1930s rather than launching any attack on capitalism. It has been claimed that Tasmanian Labor philosophy was a mixture of Henry Georgism 'and vague forms of Christian socialism'.[15]

Sectarian politics in New South Wales

In New South Wales there was increased Catholic involvement in the Labor Party with the expulsion of many of its non-Catholic members in 1916 for supporting conscription. The proportion of Catholics in the parliamentary party grew from 35% in 1913 to 61% in 1922, but ranging from lapsed to devout Catholics, they were not a unified block. A radical example was Jack Lang, an anti-capitalist socialist who regarded his Catholic faith, in which he was often negligent, as strictly part of his private life. One reason suggested for Lang joining the Labor Party was that he and the other New South Wales Catholic politicians joined because of its general social and economic philosophy which reflected their low socio-economic origins.[16] However, according to Lang himself, religion was part of that philosophy. He argued in 1928 that 'all theories of the equitable distribution of wealth and for the protection of the poor and helpless are fundamentally based on the Sermon on the Mount'.[17] This was in response to charges that his socialism was Communist. His reply also suggests a religious reason for his strident opposition to Communism. The social conscience of Lang's colleague Peter Loughlin, a devout Catholic, was definitely influenced by his religious faith.

There was no unified 'Catholic' position in debates within the New South Wales Labor Party other than opposition to the sectarianism of their non-Labor opponents. Under the reign of the unimaginative and at times timorous Kelly, who was Archbishop from 1911 to 1940, there was no attempt to organise a Catholic parliamentary block. Some priests founded the Catholic Federation in Sydney in 1913, but it had little influence on the Labor Party's steadfast opposition to state aid for Catholic schools and hospitals. Reacting to this failure and to the growing influence of socialism within the party, in 1919 the Federation launched the Democratic Party. But it had little impact in the 1920 election, won by Labor. The Democrats did win one seat in the 1922 election, but that was under the favourable conditions for minor parties in a new multi-member electoral system, and the party still had little wider electoral support. Most Catholics still voted Labor.

By contrast, there was strong Protestant influence in non-Labor parties in inter-war New South Wales. Catholics were virtually disbarred from the National and Progressive Parties in the early 1920s. Leading members of Protestant churches and temperance organisations were influential members. One was Thomas Ley, a leading parliamentary member of the Progressive Party and later a Nationalist Minister, who had been prominent in temperance and Presbyterian organisations and who impressed many people with his community work and pious speeches. However, he was also a murderer, for which he was later convicted in England.

Ley and other Progressive and Nationalist Protestant politicians played a vicious sectarian game in the 1922 New South Wales state election. A catalyst was a notorious affair in the previous year, when Bridget Partridge, a thirty-one-year-old nun named Mary Ligouri, fled from her convent in the New South Wales provincial city of Wagga. She was then pursued by Catholic clergy and laity, arrested and released from a charge of insanity, and temporarily kidnapped by her brother. She was then protected by Loyal Orange Lodge members and by a Congregational clergy family. There was a sensational trial during which lurid details of convent life were exposed, when Bridget unsuccessfully sued Wagga's Bishop Joseph Dwyer for wrongful arrest. Exaggerated accounts of her ordeals became lethal ammunition for Protestant politicians to fire in a vigorous anti-Catholic campaign in the 1922 election. A related issue was the *Ne Temere* Papal decree of 1908 against mixed marriages. It was being enforced in Australia against some Catholics who married Protestants outside Catholic churches, though many escaped ignominy, such as the future Labor Prime Minister, Ben Chifley, a devout Catholic who had married his wife, Elizabeth, in a Presbyterian church. Also the previous appearance of the Democratic Party had aroused exaggerated fears of a Catholic threat to Protestant social and political supremacy.

A Protestant Labor Party emerged in Newcastle in 1922, and its leader, Methodist lay preacher Walter Skelton, topped the poll. A prominent Nationalist member of the Protestant Federation and former Methodist minister, John Lee, headed the poll in a safe Labor seat in Sydney. Labor lost the election decisively, with its vote falling to only 38.5%, though some of the lost votes went to the Democratic Party.

The subsequent coalition government of Progressives and Nationalists tried to keep the fires of sectarianism alive. However, their plans went awry when Ley pressed for a bill to declare any imputation against the validity of lawful marriage an offence subject to a fine of £100 or two years' gaol. The bill ran into trouble in the Legislative Council which contained some men of legal stature, such as Sir John Hughes, an influential solicitor and a lone Catholic in the National Party. He delivered a temperate speech emphasising that the bill was an attack on freedom of religious opinion, claiming that actual Catholic pressure against mixed marriages was isolated, and warning the house 'not to make the mistake of yielding to a wave of sectarian feeling'.[18] The bill still passed, but in an amended form which emasculated its power. It had aroused significant opposition among Protestant churches, which were divided on the issue as a sign of widespread public concern about an attack on religious freedom.

Sectarianism consequently played a much less prominent role in the 1925 New South Wales election. A better organised Protestant Labor Party polled 19% of the vote in Newcastle, but fared much worse elsewhere. Safe Labor seats lost in 1922 to ultra-Protestants were regained. Sectarianism was on its way out of New South Wales politics.

Non-sectarian federal politics

The diminution of political sectarianism was soon demonstrated on the Australian federal scene. In 1928, Labor won office led by John Scullin, who became the first Catholic Prime Minister of

Australia. In the election campaign there was much less sectarianism employed against him and the Labor Party than was used in the same year against the first Catholic major-party American Presidential candidate, Al Smith. Scullin's concern for social justice had been influenced by his devout Catholic faith, and he had been a convinced socialist, though moderating his radicalism by 1928. He headed a federal party in which there were initially very few Catholics — only 8% in 1901 — but which grew to 22% in 1916 before the conscription crisis. Only four of the twenty-five members leaving the party on the conscription issue were Catholic, so the Catholic proportion of the smaller remnant of Labor members rose. Also, 49% of that party's members elected from 1917 to 1930 were Catholics.[19] So, whereas there had been only one or two Catholics in previous federal Labor Governments, in Scullin's Cabinet they were a majority.

However, the Catholics in the federal Labor Party did not push for specific Catholic policies. This was partly because the Commonwealth had no direct responsibility for education and health. Nor in the inter-war years was there any indication of religious loyalty influencing divisions within that party.

Certainly, the 1931 split in the federal Labor Party was caused by the impact of the depression which descended on Australia in 1929 rather than by any religious division. Lyons and his followers defected because of concern about the Cabinet's deviations from economic orthodoxy. Lang caused a split in New South Wales Labor ranks with his populist opposition to the economic austerity accepted by the Scullin Government under pressure from overseas creditors, conservative bankers and the non-Labor controlled Senate. Lang's refusal to pay interest on his government's British debt triggered a crisis that led to his dismissal by the State Governor in an atmosphere of mounting class conflict hysteria.

There was also a movement of Catholics away from Labor by the 1930s, influenced by the fact that at this stage the old working class preponderance of Catholics was diminishing. Though 'the old school tie' favoured the graduates of elite Protestant church schools in employment prospects and there were job notices saying 'no Catholics may apply', such religious prejudice had not been strong enough in Australia to threaten seriously the social mobility of Catholics. The advent of Labor governments encouraged Catholic dominance of public services. Economic expansion had given enough opportunities for enterprising Catholics to form their own business ventures, and there were numerous Protestant firms that did not discriminate against Catholics. Consequently, by 1933 11% of Catholic male breadwinners were in the top income bracket, earning £260 or more per annum, which was not far behind the 14% of Anglicans, though more so than the 16% of Methodists and 19% of Presbyterians. The national average was 13%. In those depressed times, 22% of Catholic males were unemployed, but so too were 19% of Anglicans and 15% of Methodists and Presbyterians. Also, nearly as many male Catholics (7.6%) as Anglicans (8.2%) were employers.[20]

In fact anti-Catholicism was not a significant feature of the federal non-Labor parties, though like their State counterparts they were heavily Protestant. Their mind-set was displayed when the Nationalist Minister for Defence from 1923 to 1925, Eric Bowden, who was a Methodist local preacher, declared: 'This is a Protestant country'.[21] However, of the non-Labor members elected to the Commonwealth Parliament from 1901 to 1947, 7% were Catholics. Significantly, only one of them represented a city electorate. Their rural electorates were especially regions with some Catholic strength, such as Eden-Monaro and Hume in southeastern New South Wales. However, anti-Catholicism did not enter into the consideration of the non-Labor power brokers who in 1931 offered Lyons the leadership of the new United Australia Party (UAP). Indeed, it was hoped that Lyons would attract Catholic support for the new party.

The acceptance of some Catholics in non-Labor ranks was influenced by the development among elite Protestants of a civic reform and community consensus outlook. This ideology was attached emotionally to the British Empire, but it also deplored class and religious divisions in society. It was exemplified by the Round Table, an empire-wide movement concerned about the relations between Britain and the self-governing dominions. Its Australian journal, *Round Table*, commented approvingly that the Nationalist Government's campaign in the 1925 federal election 'was free from embarrassment of sectarian questions'.[22] The Round Table's Australian membership included prominent academics and other leading figures of the public service and business worlds. Practically all were Protestants, some church-attenders and others lapsed. Their reform values were similar to the civic reform policies of the Progressive movement prior to the First World War in the United States. American Progressivism had been similarly White Anglo-Saxon Protestant, though more aggressively moralistic, as in its contribution to the victory in 1920 of complete prohibition of alcoholic drink.

The absence of moral fervour among the Australian inter-war civic reform elite represented a waning religious influence. While practically all of its members would have been baptised and married in churches, and most would have attended non-government Protestant secondary schools, an acknowledgement of the public value of religion rather than any religious enthusiasm was a major characteristic. An example was Richard Casey, who at the age of forty, after serving Australia as an external affairs advisor in Britain, entered the federal Parliament as a UAP member in 1931 and was Treasurer from 1935 to 1939. He was baptised an Anglican and educated at the Melbourne Church of England Grammar School. But there is nothing to suggest that he had any religious fervor or was even a believer. He had to face some sectarianism in his push to become the UAP candidate in the Corio electorate in Geelong because his Irish name reflected Catholic ancestry. However, he won that battle and became a determined opponent of any use of sectarianism in the UAP and its Liberal Party successor.

Protestantism and fascism

Some Protestants reacted to the industrial turmoil of the 1920s and the depression of the 1930s in anti-democratic ways by supporting fascist political groups. The two most significant were the 'New Guard' and the 'All for Australia League' in New South Wales, founded in 1931 to oppose the allegedly Communist Lang government, and advocating the abandonment of parliamentary government. Eric Campbell, the principal founder of the New Guard, was a Presbyterian Freemason. Robert Gillespie, founder of its neo-fascist predecessor, the 'Old Guard', was a Presbyterian elder. One of the speakers at the rally forming the All for Australia League was Sydney's leading Congregationalist minister, Thomas Ruth. There was also broader clerical support for the fascist values of these movements. In February 1930 the Sydney Anglican journal, *Church Standard*, welcomed a comment by a prominent Anglican layman that a government of notables from outside parliament 'would go far to cleanse the public life of the state'.[23]

Nevertheless, the fascist groups had little electoral impact. Only a small minority of Protestant churchmen gave them public support.

Much wind was taken out of their militant sails by the sacking of Lang. Later, Campbell's attempt to organise a Centre Party was a miserable failure. Though the All for Australia League cooperated in the formation of the UAP, its advocacy of restricting the franchise prevented it from having any significant influence in that party.

Churches and the Great Depression

Though many Protestants regarded the fascist movements as too extreme, they demonstrated their innate conservatism in their reactions to the Great Depression. There was widespread support among the Protestant churches for the conservative economic prescription of retrenchment. The churches deplored the recklessness of over-borrowing in the past and called for a spiritual revival. They also accepted the non-Labor propaganda that the Scullin Government had been financially irresponsible. Lang's attempts to repudiate the British debt exacerbated the apprehension of Labor Party threats to financial rectitude. The devoutly Methodist Victorian academic, Georgina Sweet, emphasised the danger to the nation's soul, when in 1931 at a rally organised by the Australian Council of Women, she moved a motion: 'that the restoration of national credit by sound finance and administration is vital to the interests of Australia'.[24]

In their reaction to the depression, church spokesmen insisted that they were not being political. The Anglican Archbishop of South Australia, Nutter Thomas, claimed that his church did not endorse any party platform. However, when the Scullin Government lost the December 1931 election, he issued a pastoral letter which, quoting Isaiah, declared: 'in the past year we have walked in darkness ... But there came to the fore men of conviction and honour'.[25] Other clergy eschewed such public comments but had firm private political views, such as the New South Wales Presbyterian minister, W. J. Grant, who wrote to a friend in 1932: 'Did you hear that Lang's party was ousted last Saturday and that a party standing for honesty and decency is in power?'[26] These views reflected the middle class nature of the Protestant clergy and laity. A continuing strong attachment to Britain also encouraged Protestants to condemn Lang's debt-repudiation policy.

Furthermore, the Nationalists and the UAP used moral and religious themes freely in their political propaganda. Repudiation of Australia's financial obligations to Britain would destroy the country's 'moral fibre'. 'Prodigality' in the preceding decade was the cause of depression. A regeneration of 'spiritual values' was required. The parties appealed blatantly to church-attending voters with advertisements such as: 'Vote for the safe party, the Home party, the solid man who believes in Religion, Christian Marriage, Christian Ideals, Christian Morality'.[27] There were of course other themes in these parties' propaganda with their appeals to British Empire loyalty, their fixation against government economic intervention, and their vigorous exploitation of anti-Communism.

However, in the 1930s there were greater efforts by churches than in the 1890s to extend helping hands to the unemployed. St John's Anglican Church in Canberra provided food, clothing and Christmas gifts for the camps of unemployed people in the nation's capital. The Presbyterian church in Melbourne's elite suburb of Toorak provided food for the parish's South Richmond mission to distribute to the unemployed. In Richmond, a working class suburb, the Salvation Army, as elsewhere, was in the forefront of feeding the near-starving along with the Ladies' Benevolent Society, most of whose members were church-attending Protestants. South Australian Methodists also sent food and other goods to six circuit missions for distribution to the unemployed.

Such good works, however, were essentially palliative. Though taking seriously the Biblical injunction to feed the hungry and clothe the naked, their emphasis was the extension of helping hands to unfortunate individuals, rather than to question whether the social system was responsible for the depression. Also, the moral fervour and middle class background of most church-going Protestants made them suspicious about creating slothful dependency. There was a keenness to support relief work, such as the Methodist Brotherhood (Relief) Committee in Sydney, which sought money and job offers from wealthy Methodists to engage the unemployed in casual work. Methodists who called for higher taxes received little support. There was general church approval for cutting wages, which had a much more savage impact on the poor than on the wealthy.

Church attempts to find longer term solutions to the problem of employment were few. One approach was the establishment of Kuitpo Colony by Methodist minister Samuel Forsyth in South Australia. In its time this institution taught 7000 unemployed men basic agricultural skills — its slogan was 'not charity but chance'. Another innovative approach was taken by the Sydney Anglican priest Robert

Hammond, who had long experience helping victims of society. He established, with the support of the State Governor and businesses, 110 unemployed families on small blocks of land in the community of Hammondville beyond Sydney's outer suburb of Liverpool. However, Kuitpo and Hammondville were both seeking solutions to the unemployment problem within the existing economic system. Their solutions also reflected past emphases on the virtues of rural life as a reaction to the problems of industrialisation.

Indeed, only a few Protestants questioned the role of capitalism in the depression. One was Ernest Burgmann, Warden of St John's Anglican theological college at Morpeth, near the city of Newcastle in New South Wales. Raised in a simple bush home and with a questioning mind, he publicly criticised his church as 'tamed through the ages by the class to which she belonged'.[28] He viewed the cause of the depression as the corruption of the capitalist class and considered that the retrenchment policies of conservative governments were akin to 'faith healing'. He was saddened that the Labor Party, from which should come hope, was self-destructing in internal squabbles. For these views Burgmann was damned by Anglican colleagues as a Communist. He did support socialist policies, but he sought to transform capitalism into a cooperative alliance of all classes. He actively supported the Communist-influenced Unemployed Workers' Union, defended families evicted from their homes and lobbied, unsuccessfully, for doubling the value of the dole for the unemployed.

Burgmann had some close allies, especially his St John's subwarden, Roy Lee. He was also part of a broader group of Anglicans influenced by British Christian socialism and by the Tractarian movement which encouraged the church's involvement in society. In New South Wales this group included Bishops Horace Crotty of Bathurst and John Moyes of Armidale, some priests, such as John Hope of Christ Church, St Laurence, and some lay academics at Sydney University. They agreed that the church must be freed from its identity with capitalism, an economic system needing fundamental reform. However, their prescriptions for change varied from Crotty, who for a time was attracted by New Guard ideas, to a few socialists like Hope and Burgmann. Also the social reform movement was a distinct minority within the Church of England and met much resistance. Nevertheless, despite Burgmann's reputation as 'a rabid socialist', he was elected in 1934 as the Bishop of Goulburn, with the assistance of a few priests who were his ex-students, with the crucial support of a senior member of the diocese who had been attracted by Burgmann's proposal to double the dole, and with the help of two rival candidates who cancelled each other out.

Among some other Protestant clergy the depression sharpened more critical thought about the world capitalist order. One was John Lawton, a Victorian Presbyterian minister and former travelling secretary of the Australian Student Christian Movement (ASCM), who founded a Movement Towards a Christian Social Order. But most of his fellow Presbyterians were not moved to question the capitalist economy. In the Victorian Methodist Church there were a few who responded to the depression with Christian socialist attitudes, notably Oswald Barnett. He was a prominent advocate for releasing the poor from the crowded and squalid housing conditions of Melbourne's slums and was influential in the establishment of the Victorian Housing Commission in 1938. But though influenced by the radical strand of Methodism that had prompted past Methodist support for trade unionism and the Labor Party, Barnett was criticised for 'pro-Communism' by some of the majority conservative clergy and laity in his church.

Barnett's type of radicalism was to have a greater impact on postwar Protestants. In universities, the ASCM was challenging Christian students to reflect critically about the social evils of the age and to apply Christian social gospel principles to these issues. Future community leaders were being influenced by social criticism at some Christian private schools. At the elite Melbourne Church of England Girls Grammar School, one of its students in the 1930s, the later notable educationist, Gwyneth Dow, commented that the school had a 'very strong sense of social injustice'.[29] At Scotch College, the leading Presbyterian boys' school in Melbourne, a chaplain, the Rev. Steve Yarnold, was a self-confessed Christian socialist. He had a lasting influence on radical social thinking among some of his middle class students who were to become future church and community leaders.

However, there were limits to the radicalism encouraged by Church private schools. This is demonstrated by Janet McCalman's recent study of members of the 1930s generation of students at Scotch College, the Methodist Ladies College (MLC), the Church of England's second-ranking Melbourne boys' school, Trinity College, and the Catholic girls' convent, Genazzano, who still lived in the late 1980s in the middle class suburbs of eastern Melbourne. These schools encouraged a spirit of public service and social responsibility among many of their students, which helped provide the social welfare side of post-war political conservatism. Only 2.3% of the Scotch students ended up as Christian socialists and another 4.5% as secular socialists. There were smaller percentages of socialist graduates of the other schools, except the 2.5% of Christian socialists among those attending Genazzano. Most of the graduates of all schools were in the 'middle-of-the road' and small 'l' liberal political categories. One-fifth of the MLC students and more than a quarter of the others were conservatives. Of those who expressed a party political preference, supporters of the Liberal Party outnumbered Labor supporters by more than four to one of Scotch and Genazzano graduates, and by more than three to one of those attending Trinity and MLC.[30]

Social justice thinking existed within the Catholic church, but the main Catholic response to the depression of the 1930s was similar to the majority Protestant emphasis on feeding, clothing and housing the destitute unemployed. In Western Australia, the church saw its role as dispensing charity, exemplified by the work of the St. Vincent de Paul Society. It also campaigned for more unity and cooperation between classes as an antidote to socialism. In Brisbane, Duhig took a further step by arranging for the establishment of hundreds of unemployed Catholic youths on the land, but this program was no more radical than the Protestant work of Forsyth and Hammond.

The most significant Catholic challenge to the capitalist system arose in Melbourne. There a group of young university-educated laymen responded to the Pope's 1931 encyclical *Quadragesimo Anno*, which called for active lay participation through Catholic Action groups in the affairs of the modern world. The Melbourne Catholic Action group called themselves 'Catholic social revolutionaries'. In 1936, with the support of Mannix, who laid the blame for Ireland's problems at the door of British capitalism, they launched the radical *Catholic Worker*, edited by the intellectually gifted Bartholomew A. M. Santamaria. In the journal's first editorial, he wrote that the 'exalted position of Public Enemy No. 1 is reserved for Capitalism', not Communism. Catholics should have no sympathy for capitalism, 'which has de-christianised the world by its insistence on secular education; which has sacrificed the Home on the altar of the Machine; which has deprived the ordinary man of property and has destroyed his liberty'.[31] Whilst anti-capitalist, in that statement were the ingredients of a pre-capitalist and corporatist ideology, in line with the ideal of a cooperative social order expressed in *Quadragesimo Anno*. By-products were an admiration for Mussolini's fascist regime in Italy and support for Franco's fascist nationalists in the Spanish Civil War.

Indeed, there was strong Australian Catholic sympathy for Franco, which was influenced by propaganda about Communist control of the Spanish Republican Government. Students at Genazzano remember watching newsreels about Spain with the nuns telling them, 'Now girls, you must all clap for General Franco'.[32] In this political climate the leader of the federal Labor Party, John Curtin, kept quiet about his support for the Republicans for fear of splitting the party. Indeed, there were heated disputes about the Spanish Civil War between Catholics and left wing socialists at trade union and Labor Party congresses.

Jews and anti-semitism

Another impact of the depression was a small increase in anti-semitism in Australia. The Jewish proportion of the population in Australia had never been large: 0.5% in 1861 and 0.4% in 1933. However, Jews had a disproportionate influence in Australia because of their wealth and education and their concentration in urban regions, particularly in Melbourne and Sydney. Since early days of self-government, Jews had been members of Parliament, such as Ephraim Zox, who was in the Victorian Legislative Assembly from 1877 to 1899 and Daniel Levy, who was Speaker of the New South Wales Legislative Assembly from 1919 to 1932. Many leading Jews were prominent members of the Australian business world, such as Sydney company director and financial wizard George Judah Cohen and Simcha Baevski, a Russian immigrant, who became Sydney Myer, the founder of Melbourne's great retail emporium. Significantly, 29% of Jewish breadwinners were in the top income bracket in 1933, well ahead of all other religious groups except a similar proportion of Unitarians and 33% of the members of Strong's Australian Church.[33]

In Australia prior to the 1930s, Jews had faced little overt discrimination. However, there was an underlying anti-semitism expressed in the cartoons of the *Bulletin* and *Smith's Weekly*, where Jews were often depicted as pedlars, crafty businessmen and bloated capitalists. In the early Labor Party, Jews were identified with exploitative capitalism, exemplified in the novel by the secularist Frank Anstey, *Kingdom of Shylock*, published in 1915. Jews were blackballed from some elite Australian social institutions, such as the Melbourne Club and the

Royal Sydney Golf Club. However, the fact that most of the nineteenth century Jewish settlers in Australia came from Britain, even if born elsewhere, made it easy for Jews to meld into the colonial community, eliminating any major discrimination. Also, at the end of the First World War the prestige of Australian Jewry rose with accolades poured on Australia's leading General, John Monash, whose Jewishness was no barrier to his progression to that rank and in his later appointment as General Manager of the Victorian State Electricity Commission. In high honours, Monash was to be eclipsed by a fellow Victorian Jew, Isaac Isaacs. He was a Cabinet member and Acting Premier of Victoria, a Federal Attorney-General, a judge and Chief Justice of the High Court of Australia and, from 1931 to 1936, the first locally-born Governor-General of Australia. However, in conservative circles, after the Russian revolution, Jews who had migrated from eastern Europe were often seen as Bolsheviks and revolutionaries. In the 1920s there was some separation in Christian Australian thought between 'good Jews' who were Anglicised like Monash and Isaacs, and 'bad Jews' from continental Europe.

In the 1930s, this latent anti-semitism in Australia was fed by the effects of depression and by developments in Europe. In the fascist groups in Australia there was an undercurrent of anti-semitism. The Guild of Watchmen in South Australia, which applauded the rise of the Nazi Party to power in Germany, introduced to Australia the infamous Czarist hoax, *The Protocols of the Elders of Zion*, which detailed the alleged Zionist conspiracy to rule the world. The Australia First Movement in Sydney launched vicious attacks against 'Semitism' in its journal the *Publicist*. There were also expressions of anti-semitism among Catholics, especially among those who admired Mussolini. In 1936 the Australian Catholic Truth Society published *The Truth About Freemasonry*, in which it described the alleged large role of 'Masonic Jews' in dominating Australia's economy. The *Freeman's Journal* articulated the feelings of many Catholics that international Jewry controlled news services which distorted events in Germany, Italy and Spain. But, unlike Europe, there were no physical attacks on Jews or Jewish establishments. The very limited appeal of fascism in Australia, the previous ready acceptance of Jewish citizens, and the smallness of the Jewish communities, enabled Jews to enjoy more freedom from anti-semitism in Australia in the 1930s than in most other countries of the world.

One area where the prejudice against potentially 'bad' foreign Jews had an impact was in Australia's reluctance to allow immigration of Jewish refugees from continental Europe. Australian Quakers, responding to efforts by the London Society of Friends to facilitate the emigration of Jews from Germany, placed pressure on the Australian Government to accept these and other refugees from Germany and Austria. Prominent in this work was Camilla Wedgwood, an anthropologist who was a convert to Quakerism. Initially, she felt 'like a mouse nibbling at a mountain' in trying to move the Australian Government to abandon its fixation on Anglo-Saxon homogeneity.[34] In 1938, after the Austrian Anschluss (the German takeover of Austria) and Kristallnacht (a night of Nazi destruction of Jewish property), which focused more international attention on the plight of Germany's Jews, Australia was pressed by its High Commissioner in London, Stanley Bruce, to take 30 000 refugees over three years. Australia agreed to take only half that number, four-fifths of whom could be Jewish, as long as each migrant could be suitably integrated into Australian society.

Paternalism and Aboriginal missions

Paternalism continued to be the general style of missionary work with Aborigines in twentieth-century Australia until after the Second World War. This was the case with the Aborigines Inland Mission (AIM), founded in 1905 and the United Aborigines Mission (UAM), formed in 1929 from two other groups. By 1944 these evangelical Protestant interdenominational missions accounted for nearly half of all Christian missionaries working with Aborigines. Many of these missionaries were dedicated people, at times living on the fringes of country towns in conditions little better than those of the Aborigines themselves. In 1916 several women AIM missionaries in the Singelton district in New South Wales were described as living in 'hot, patched-up structures (comprising every sort, size and kind of old timber and sheet iron) without the least comfort'.[35] These missionaries generally were remembered with affection by Aborigines who came into contact with them. But James Miller, whose older relatives remembered missionaries in the Singleton region, wrote that they 'accepted the poor state of things too readily. To them poverty was a test of their own faith in God, but to the Kooris it meant that they had to continue to rely on government and private charity'.[36]

Moreover, there were harsher words for missionaries involved in government-controlled reserves and institutions for Aborigines. Jimmy Barker, who in 1912 at the age of twelve, was forced by the 1911 New South Wales revision of the *Aborigines Protection Act* into the Aboriginal reserve of Brewarrina on the Darling River in northern New South Wales, remembered a preacher-teacher, Mr. Foster, who assisted in 'hammering our inferiority into us all day and every day' with frequent use of corporal punishment. Barker spoke of visiting preachers who subjected Aboriginal beliefs to 'ridicule' and insisted that 'we were useless humans and must forget our Aboriginal religion and learn all they taught us'.[37]

Also the AIM and UAM participated in a rampant practice, especially in New South Wales, of forcibly removing children from Aboriginal families to be raised in institutions or foster homes in order to integrate them into the white community. This practice continued until the early 1960s. Standards of treatment of those children greatly varied. But John Harris, who spoke to hundreds of Aboriginal people with these experiences writes that 'memories of regimentation and oppression run as a common thread through the majority of their stories'.[38] There was also an expectation that the graduates of such 'care' should be bonded out to menial service as female domestic servants and male indentured labourers. In 1916 Frances Garnett, a missionary at Point Pearce government mission in South Australia, spoke for most of her Christian colleagues when she told a Royal Commission that 'compulsory systematic placing' of mission girls in domestic service 'as they reach a suitable age' was a necessity. She further stated that since it would be too expensive 'to train them for cooking and dressmaking' and 'because there is such a demand' for unskilled domestic labour, 'they can all wash dishes and scrub floors'.[39]

There were still missionary champions who abhored the continued mistreatment of Aborigines living outside mission settlements. A major critic was Ernest Gribble who moved, at the request of the local bishop, to the Anglican mission at Forrest River in 1913, where the Western Australian Government had established an Aboriginal reserve in an attempt to stop confrontations between Aborigines and pastoralists. Gribble soon built up a thriving mission with his kindness to the indigenous people and with the help of an Aboriginal couple from Yarrabah, James and Angela Noble. However, his hope that the mission would become a safe refuge was dashed when in June 1922 a police posse searching for cattle killers entered the reserve and killed a large number of its people. The outraged Gribble sought a government enquiry without success. Then part of the reserve was taken over for soldier settlement with resulting violence on both sides of the racial divide. A consequence in 1926 was another massacre of many Aborigines following the killing of one of the settlers, Frederick Hay, after a confrontation between him and an Aborigine, Lumbuumbia. The catalyst in the affray was probably Hay's attempted abduction of an Aboriginal woman, one of the most common causes of violence on the frontiers of Australian settlement. Gribble, who cooperated with the police in the search for Lumbuumbia, again was horrified at the killing of every Aboriginal adult male the police could round up. Women and children were clubbed to death. His publicising of this outrage aroused the enmity of the white people of the town of Wyndham, who responded by ostracising his mission. This time a royal commission was appointed and two police were accused of murder. But the 'disappearance' of key witnesses and the solidarity of the people of Wyndham resulted in these police being acquitted for acting in self-defence.

This failure embittered Gribble, making his paternalistic rule over the Aboriginal people in his mission more authoritarian. When the anthropologist and Anglican priest, Adolphus Peter Elkin, visited the mission in 1927, he wrote: 'I rather feel that there is too much repression and, I regret to say, a little terrorising in the attitude ... towards the inmates'.[40] Elkin's report led to Gribble's dismissal in 1928. His authoritarianism had become too strong even for the paternalistic Anglican Australian Board of Missions (ABM).

However, even Elkin acted in an ultimately paternalistic way towards Aborigines. He had a burning mission to stop the murder and other abuses of Aborigines. His research trips in the Kimberlies and in South Australia gave him a deep appreciation of the dignity of Aborigines, a horror at the way white men abused Aboriginal women, and dismay at the wrecks of Aboriginal humanity hanging around the edges of white settlements. He also was critical about the disparagement of Aboriginal culture by Christian missionaries. With further academic research into the history of white–Aboriginal contacts since 1788, Elkin came to the conclusion that much of the observed inability of Aborigines to cope with European society was because of their own deeply embedded nomadic culture, which had a unique value and was well worth preserving.

However, Elkin accepted the prevalent 'scientific' evidence of the smaller size of Aboriginal brains and a Darwinian explanation for the decline of the Aboriginal population as a species frozen in time by its isolation and therefore unable to adapt to European culture. His proposal was to appoint an anthropologically-trained administrator for all Aborigines in northern and central Australia with patrol officers who would gradually build up a body of culturally appropriate law. His model was Australia's colony of Papua which, under its staunchly Catholic Lieutenant-Governor, Hubert Murray, was receiving worldwide acclaim as an ideal colony, but which had a heavily paternalistic administration. Under such government guidance, Aborigines would be protected and gradually prepared to live in a European dominated Australia, though their culture would be preserved. However, this program was presented in an authoritarian style, expecting people to accept his prescription for a sick Aboriginal society without explanation.

In his roles as Professor of Anthropology at Sydney University and as the President for the Association for the Protection of Native Races (APNR), Elkin did have significant influence on Commonwealth Government Aboriginal policies which affected the Northern Territory only. An early example was the spearing to death in 1933 of Constable Stewart McColl while hunting for the murderers of five Japanese trepang collectors and two European prospectors at Caledon Bay in Arnhem Land in the Northern Territory. The enraged white community in Darwin provoked the Commonwealth Government administrator to organise a posse of Darwin citizens to teach the Aborigines 'a lesson'. Elkin and the secretary of the APNR, a Congregationalist minister, William Morely, sprang into action by bombarding the press and the Commonwealth Minister of the Interior about the threat of another wholesale massacre of Aborigines. Fortuitously, there was a new Minister, John Perkins. He was an active Anglican who was determined to learn about the Aboriginal problem and to restrain punitive reprisals, in contrast to the complacent attitude of his predecessor. Perkins responded to the APNR pressure by sending the requested arms for the posse by a slow sea route. Also Elkin's suggestion that Anglican Church Missionary Society (CMS) missionaries be asked to find the murderers was accepted, with resultant success.

But new battles emerged with subsequent trials of the culprits. Elkin and the APNR, with public support, persuaded Perkins to commute death sentences imposed on three Aborigines accused of murdering the Japanese and Europeans. There was also a sensational trial of Constable McColl's killer, Taukier, whose defence that McColl had interfered with Aboriginal women was lampooned by Judge T.A. Wells. Elkin responded by addressing a huge public meeting in Sydney on the question of justice for tribal Aborigines. The result was that Taukier's case was transferred by Perkins to a higher court, which declared Wells's handling of the case a miscarriage of justice and allowed Taukier his freedom. But the Darwin white community had its revenge when he disappeared on his way to rejoin his tribe.

In 1934 Elkin had another influence on Northern Territory policy in the appointment of the first territorial patrol officer, Donald Thomson, who had carried out anthropological research among Aborigines in north Queensland. In 1939 Elkin achieved a further triumph when, after convincing the bluff straight-talking Country Party Minister, Jack McEwan, he influenced the government's *Policy with respect to the Aborigines*, which his biographer describes as 'pure Elkin'.[41]

However, the position of Aborigines in the pre-Second World War Northern Territory indicated the limits of Elkin's influence and the effect of wider church apathy. In that territory, which was under Federal Government control after 1911, even the administration of justice was blatantly racist. Judge Wells disparaged and misled Aboriginal witnesses, distorted the evidence of Europeans supporting Aborigines, and constantly acquitted white abusers of Aboriginal rights. Abusers included many employers who avoided paying any wages to Aborigines and treated brutally, even murdered, their labourers without fear of judicial punishment. The economic power of pastoralists was a major barrier to implementation of government reforms in Aboriginal affairs, and Elkin and the APNR never succeeded in calls to remove Wells, who remained as Chief Justice of the territory until 1952.

Elkin also had awkward relations with the Anglican ABM. It resented his superior tone and parted company with his support for the survival of Aboriginal culture and spirituality. The ABM was locked into its identification of spirituality as Christianity with European culture.

Eurocentric Christianity was also still the world view of the other Protestant missions in the territory — Methodist and Lutheran. They were alert to atrocities committed against Aborigines, but the attention of the most vociferous church critics was centred on checking rampant abuses rather than on drawing attention to miserable living conditions, non-payment of wages, and the segregation of Aborigines from white facilities. One South Australian Presbyterian critic of mission work, Dr Charles Duguid, was surprised to learn on a visit to Alice Springs in 1934 that his own church's Australian Inland Mission, founded by the later celebrated John Flynn, concentrated on serving white settlers rather than Aborigines who were tolerated in the town only as 'hewers of wood and drawers of water' and lived in deplorably squalid conditions. When he tackled Flynn about the mission neglect, Duguid was admonished that he was 'wasting his time among so many damned, dirty niggers'.[42] A Methodist Aboriginal lobbyist, Victorian-born William Cooper, who tried vainly to convince governments in the 1920s and 1930s to grant social services, electoral enfranchisement and land rights to Aboriginal people, also met with an apathetic response from urban Christians. He wrote to Gribble in 1938: 'I did not get any sympathy from the church people here in Melbourne. The government and our Christians are very dull on [the Aboriginal] question'.[43]

In fact, in the inter-war years in the Northern Territory and other frontier regions of Australia, missions were much more concerned about saving individual Aboriginal souls than working for social justice for the Aboriginal race. This matched the church's philanthropic approach to the impact of the Great Depression in white Australia. An example of the general mission approach was the attitude of four missionaries — two Methodists and the other two representing the Anglican ABM and the Catholic missions — at a conference in the Northern Territory in 1930 about wages for Aborigines. Three union representatives at the conference moved to implement in the Territory the award wage for Aborigines in Queensland, which had been introduced by the Labor Government there, but which was only half the wage rate for whites. The mission representatives opposed the move. The Methodist Rev. Jarvis maintained that Aborigines in the Northern Territory were less developed than the products of the Queensland reserves. He argued that 'the native, practically speaking, is a child' and that giving him money would be as harmful as allowing 'my boy of five to play around with my razor'.[44] The mission representatives made common cause with the three pastoralist members of the conference which duly passed a motion recommending the provision of food and lodgings to Aboriginal workers as the substitution for wages.

It is true that, generally, better food and shelter were provided at mission stations, but they served only a minority of Aborigines. A government survey in 1941 estimated that across northern Australia 13000 Aborigines and part-Aborigines were on 'supervised' stations and 23000 others were still living a traditional life style.[45] At the time there were more than 80000 people of Aboriginal descent in Australia.

However, there were some glimmers of hope for a better mission approach in the future. In 1937 in Sydney a conference of the National Missionary Council of Australia (NMCA), which had been established in 1926, called for the granting of reserves to separate tribes as their own territory in which they would have all rights to land use, including mining. It also urged adequate government-financed health services, a new deal for the 'deplorable' position of Aboriginal women, and better educational services to eventually equip Aborigines for participation in European society. But there was a naivety that mere resolutions would bring about the acceptance by federal and state governments and even mission boards of such resolutions. Nor did anyone suggest consulting Aborigines. This conference's most effective decision was to begin a publicity campaign in Australia's churches to improve knowledge and attitudes towards Aborigines.

The waning Protestant moral order

The inter-war years saw a decline in the grip of the Protestant moral order upon the Australian community. During the 1920s there was another push for more temperance reform, inspired by the achievement of prohibition in the United States. The Protestant-dominated New South Wales Government promised to implement a referendum on prohibition of all sales of alcoholic liquor. Initially, the responsible Minister, Ley, did not deliver on this issue in a generally inconsistent performance. Outrage from temperance groups elicited a promise by the Presbyterian Premier, George Fuller, to approve a prohibition referendum in 1928. His promise was honoured on 1 September 1928 by the next non-Labor Government, led by the practising Anglican, Thomas Bavin, even though Bavin was determined to remove sectarianism from New South Wales politics. But this referendum was lost by a decisive majority in a heavy poll. The 'yes' vote received only 29%.[46]

In the 1920s, in the most heavily Protestant State of South Australia, Methodist men and women were prominent in a push for prohibition.

But such activity, and an annual resolution of the Methodist Conference calling for prohibition, were ignored at the political level. The Liberal Party leader from 1920 to 1924 was the conservative Herbert Barwell, an active Anglican synodsman, who earned much flack from temperance organisers. That hostility was one factor causing the Liberals' defeat in 1924, though Barwell's moves to dismantle industrial legislation, and bitter rivalry between Liberals and Nationalists, were probably more important reasons. Predictably, the temperance movement received no joy from the Labor governments of the next three years and of the early years of the depression. Some support was given by the Liberal–Country Party coalition government, led by the Anglican Richard Butler, who accepted in 1929 the soft option of a referendum to close hotels on Saturday afternoons, also aimed at suppressing SP (starting price) betting in hotels on horse races. But despite strong support from the Anglican and other Protestant churches, expressed by petitions and by resolutions passed at church meetings, the bill to endorse the referendum aroused intense opposition from the powerful United Licensed Victuallers' Association and many who enjoyed SP betting. The bill was defeated in the House of Assembly by twenty-seven votes to fourteen.

This defeat induced Butler to treat moral reform with great caution when he returned as Premier in 1933. He interpreted any move to suppress drinking and gambling as electorally unpopular. The consequent wrath he aroused among Protestants, and counter-moves in Parliament to extend hotel opening hours, prompted the Methodist Church to appoint a full time superintendent of its social services department, Earnest Woollacott. He was a political lobbyist seeking to influence politicians to hold the hotel line and close the betting shops, which had opened under a new law passed by the preceding Labor government. The effort, however, was only partially successful, indicating the diminution in Protestant political influence in South Australia, which Butler had sensed. The extension of hotel hours to 10 p.m. was passed by the Legislative Council. An intense campaign to influence the fate of the bill in the lower house, including a march by over 3000 church people down Adelaide's main street, resulted in the bill's defeat by just one vote. This was a narrow victory for maintenance of a past success.

On the sabbatarian front, South Australian Protestant churches were gradually losing. On South Australian Sundays, shops, hotels, cultural and entertainment centres were closed, sporting fixtures banned, and there was no morning public transport. By the 1920s, however, the standards were slipping with many people treating the day as a holiday, with some amusement centres opening, more public transport operating and some sporting events being held in Adelaide's parklands. Catholics and Lutherans refused to join in united church appeals to preserve a Christian Sabbath. The Church of England bowed to the trend and shifted its Sunday schools from afternoons to mornings. Methodists and other nonconformists could not yet see they were losing the battle to keep Sunday as a holy day of rest.

The popularity of SP betting in inter-war Australia was a symptom of a wider hedonistic challenge to the Protestant moral order. The First World War, which had given women a taste of freedom from male employment restrictions — and which limited the supply of young men — influenced a post-war abandonment of conservative dress conventions. Hemlines rose and necklines dropped. The battle to stop the exposure of bare flesh in swimming costumes was lost. Motor cars, radio and the cinema provided new freedom and more secular values. Wider availability of birth control devices assisted new sexual liberty. Ironically, the sexual changes were fewest in the sector of the working class which aspired to 'respectability'. In Melbourne's working class suburb of Richmond many young people who still went to church, even for mere social reasons, remained pre-marital virgins if only for lack of opportunity in a non-car owning and tightly-cohesive society. Also one area where the churches held the line was censorship. Films were carefully vetted by the Commonwealth Censorship Board; books like Lawrence's *Lady Chatterley's Lover* were banned; and the press conformed to strict moral codes.

Churches were starting to lose their strong community influence. Church spokesmen still commanded media attention and were sought for moral guidance, but Protestant church attendance was sliding. Numbers attending Protestant churches in working class Richmond were falling. The many social and cultural activities of these churches had started to fade. A contrast was the Catholic Church. With its separate school system and priestly control, this church was maintaining the allegiance of its own people, enhanced by an increased siege mentality among Catholics after the conscription crisis in the preceding war. Among the middle class of Melbourne's eastern suburbs, the churches were still a central institution for most Protestants and, especially for Methodists, a centre for their social lives. Puritanical moral values still held sway in most Protestant and Catholic middle class homes. A student at MLC in the 1930s commented: 'It was not a very religious school, but it was a very moral one ... As far as I know there was only one girl who lost her virginity all the time I was there'.[47] However, a strident campaign by Catholic clergy against birth control was a sign that its practice was spreading among Catholic middle class families, which were becoming smaller in size, though still larger than those of Protestants. Also attendances at Protestant church services in this realm of respectability were slowly falling, particularly among men.

The rate of decline in church attendance cannot be measured because there were no longer any church-attendance censuses. Some other statistics, however, demonstrate it. Church membership figures hide members who did not attend worship services, but do measure the incorporation of teenage and other new members. The proportion of all Australians who were members of the two major non-Anglican Protestant churches, Methodists and Presbyterians, fell from 3.53% in 1911 to under 3.4% in 1936. A sharper decline of church influence is measured by an absolute fall in these years of children in Methodist and Presbyterian Sunday schools from 271 186 to 202 617, despite a general Australian population rise of nearly 50%. By contrast, the number of children attending Catholic schools rose from 114 893 in 1911 to 188 181 in 1936.[48]

Summary

The First World War, which Protestant clergy envisioned might be an opportunity for spiritual regeneration in Australia, proved the reverse. Protestant success during the war in shortening hotel hours was a high watermark in the campaign for a moral order in Australia. In the use of Sundays there were signs of decline matched by the beginnings of a drop in church attendance. Furthermore, renewed outbursts of sectarianism in politics were short-lived. A growth of religious tolerance was influenced by a decline in religious enthusiasm among the conservative Protestant political elite, though there was still widespread public acknowledgement of Christianity.

Also during the inter-war years the Churches demonstrated their continued conservative influence in Australia. The rising Catholic influence in Labor Parties contributed to a declining influence of anti-capitalist socialism, though never strong enough to overthrow the Labor commitment to secular education. Protestants were still much more aligned with non-Labor parties, but with now limited influence on the political implementation of moral reform. The many efforts to help the unemployed and destitute during the depression were mostly a continuation of traditional charity. Only a few clergy and active Christians were willing to criticise the capitalist system, and even fewer supported a socialist alternative. The small outburst of Catholic socialism had pre-capitalist and corporationist overtones.

The inter-war years witnessed missions continuing their paternalistic approaches to Aborigines. Even Elkin, who parted company with the ABM on the value of preserving Aboriginal culture, considered he knew best for the future of Aborigines. He and some other missionaries protested at flagrant breaches of Aboriginal rights. But there was general church neglect of the rampant economic exploitation of Aborigines.

CHAPTER FIVE

PRESERVATION OF CHRISTIAN AUSTRALIA, *1939–1960*

The Second World War did not reveal the sectarian tensions of the First World War. But it saw the beginnings of Catholic action in trade unions against Communism, with later devastating consequences for the Labor Party. Christian prescriptions for a new social order in post-war Australia were again based on the continued concern about the threatened moral order. This chapter explores these themes as well as the resilience of Christianity and Christian values in post-war Australia and new mission approaches to Aborigines.

The Second World War

When the Second World War began in 1939, there was a much more muted Australian church reaction than at the start of the First World War. The long crisis of Hitler's aggression in Europe had created a public air of resigned expectancy. On the Sunday morning of 2 September, having heard news of Germany's attack on Poland, more Australians than normal went to church services to hear preachers calling for calm and Christian fortitude. That evening, when Prime Minister Robert Menzies broadcast over radio that Australia would follow Britain in declaring war on Germany, he said it was a 'melancholy duty'. Nor on the next Sunday did clergymen respond to the news with the same jingoistic enthusiasm as in 1914. However, as in that war, there was a general church theme about the moral judgments of God which would draw all nations to a new righteousness. The Anglican bishop of Northern Queensland, John Feetham, who in the First World War had said the cost of the war could only be justified by national regeneration, summed up the common Second World War sentiment: 'God is at work in the midst of this turmoil to bring out of it a good issue'.[1]

In the 1930s there had been an Australian Christian peace movement renouncing war. This movement had been influenced by the Christian Peace Pledge movement in Britain and by a general revulsion to the slaughter of the First World War—it was also exacerbated by the trauma of the 1930s depression. A Legion of Christian Youth was founded in Australia in 1936 to work for peace. Bishop Burgmann was its president, and prominent members were the Methodist pacifist, Alan Robson, and the Presbyterian social reformer, Alan Dalziel. The Anglican travelling Secretary of the ASCM, Frank Coaldrake, edited *The Peacemaker*, devoted to discussing peace issues. Melbourne Methodist ministers Rex Mathias, Palmer Phillips and Frank Hartley promoted public discussions about peace questions. However, the growing European crisis and outbreak of war in 1939 evaporated most of this Christian advocacy of peace. Burgmann retained his detestation of war as 'totally unchristian'.[2] But he withdrew from the youth legion because of Robson's open espousal of pacifism, which Burgmann considered undesirable for the war against Hitler. He called for public cooperation with the war effort. The ASCM recognised that 'the majority' of its members 'support the war as the last practical instrument of national policy available to us'.[3]

One religious sect was persecuted and received no wider church support. Members of the small group of Jehovah's Witnesses, in January 1941, were declared a proscribed organisation for advocating pacifism. That sect lost an appeal to the High Court, which declared that the government's defence powers overrode religious rights. However, the more socially respectable Quakers continued to enjoy pacifist liberty. The socially unacceptable Communist Party was banned by the Menzies Government in 1940.

The Catholic Church did not offer any opposition to this war, including the introduction in 1942 of conscription for overseas service. Before the war the Catholic Church had supported appeasement. There also had been a growing concern about Communism which had influenced Catholic support for Franco's fascists in the Spanish Civil War. However, the German-Soviet pact of August 1939 reinforced previous Catholic opposition to Nazi Germany, which had invaded

Catholic Austria and which had elevated neo-paganist ideology. There was therefore broad Catholic support for Australia's declaration of war. Archbishop Mannix, who was more concerned about Communist Russia than Nazi Germany, justified Ireland's neutrality in the war. But the Australian-born Norman Gilroy, who was appointed Sydney's coadjutor bishop in 1937, virtually taking over from the ailing Kelly, and who became archbishop in March 1940, staunchly supported Australia's war effort from the outset. To Archbishop Duhig in Brisbane, the issues were much clearer than in 1914. It was a just war, exemplified by the unprovoked German invasion of Catholic Poland. Also with Japan's entry into the war in December 1941, Mannix supported the war effort more seriously, though after the fall of Singapore he characteristically blamed Britain for 'hollow' promises of protection that had encouraged Australia's 'groundless feeling of security'.[4]

Mannix also confronted Menzies in 1940. He threatened mass Catholic protests over the action of local authorities in Broome in northwestern Australia who imprisoned German missionary priests and brothers of the Pallotine Order, who had been working among the Aborigines of the Kimberley region. Menzies had no wish to provoke a fight with the fiery Mannix and quickly ordered the release of the prisoners.

Catholic concern about Communism grew during the war. Previously, during the 1930s, Communist influence in Australia's trade unions had increased. The unemployment and depressed wages of workers had alienated many from moderate trade union leadership and had made Marxist propaganda about how the Labor Party and the unions had sold out to rapacious capitalism more attractive. Major unions, such as the Waterside Workers' Federation and the Federated Ironworkers' Association (FIA), had come under the control of Communist leadership. Communist influence in State trade union councils also grew to the extent of capturing the Brisbane Trades and Labour Council (TLC). Catholic Labor Party politicians who were alarmed at these developments, especially Herbert Cremean, the deputy leader of the Victorian Labor Party, approached members of the Catholic Action group to assist in combatting Communism in the unions. The result was the formation in Melbourne in August 1941 of the Catholic Social Studies Movement (CSSM), with strong support from Mannix. Commonly known as 'the Movement', this organisation of lay Catholics, with the twenty-five-year-old Santamaria as its mentor, began a crusade against Communism.

In New South Wales, Catholic Labor politicians already had acted strongly to suppress a perceived upsurge of Communist influence in their party. Its annual conference in 1940 passed a 'Hands off Russia' resolution, which opposed any extension of the war against the neutral Soviet Union. The resolution was moved by leftist members, some of whom were secret Communists, and was approved partly because the anti-Communist Lang faction in the party saw it as a means of publicly discrediting the pro-Communists. Predictably, the resolution aroused a strong adverse reaction from the Catholic influenced right wing of the party as well as from the federal Labor Party, which was aghast at the potential electoral liability of the resolution. The left wing-controlled Central Executive of the New South Wales party was dismissed, and a new executive was installed pledged to support the government's war aims.

Aa a consequence of this expulsion leftist supporters of the old executive defected into a new State Labor Party, and there was also a second split with Lang's formation of the Australian Labor Party (Non Communist). Catholic influence was maintained in the official New South Wales party, which still won the 1941 state election comfortably. Though it was led by an Anglican, William McKell, eight of the eighteen new Labor members of parliament were Catholics.

However, Catholics had problems with the federal Labor Government which took office in October 1941. Prime Minister John Curtin had long abandoned his Catholic faith and in Canberra sought solace in the manse of the Presbyterian Church of St Andrews with its Labor-voting minister, Hector Harrison. While half of the other members of Curtin's first Cabinet were Catholics, one of the important Ministers, the Attorney-General, Dr Herbert Vere Evatt, had an Anglican background and no love for any of the institutional churches. Nevertheless he was happy to attempt to influence church leaders, such as Duhig, who tried to cultivate him.

Duhig became very concerned at the plans that Evatt and other members of the government were hatching for the post-war era. They were seeking more government intervention into the social and economic life of the nation. To Duhig, whose understanding of such matters was limited, this had the stench of dreaded socialism. The first battleground was a referendum in August 1944 to pass fourteen constitutional amendments to give the federal government powers of economic and social control. Duhig declared that the party was speaking with a hypocritical voice, on the one hand condemning Communism and on the other planning socialisation of industry, which was 'the chief plank of Communism'.[5] Though he insisted publicly that he had not advised people to vote 'no', he was gleeful when the negative vote triumphed. But he was even more obsessed when late in 1944 the devout Catholic Treasurer, Chifley, introduced a bill to give the Commonwealth Bank power to control private banks. Financial freedom, in his view, was essential for the independence of the church. Duhig's affair with the Labor Party was over. He now considered it had prostituted itself to socialism.

Within the Church of England during the war there was consideration about the post-war order in Australia in the form of the Christian Social Order Movement (CSOM). It had roots in earlier social gospel thought and was promoted especially by Bishop Moyes and W.G. Coughlin, rector of Holy Trinity, South Kensington in Sydney. The movement called for the Anglican Church to abandon its 'ambulance' approach to social problems and become involved in reforming the unjust structures of society. It called for a new order in which economics would be the servant of the whole community and sectional interests would be subordinated to the general good. The CSOM under Coughlan's energetic direction sought to revolutionise the Church of England to accept social responsibility as a handmaiden to evangelism. It published a newspaper and radio programs named 'New Day' and established parish study and action groups. The CSOM linked with wider community groups such as the Council of Social Services. It also campaigned in favour of a 'yes' vote in the Labor Government's 1944 constitutional powers referendum. But that political action aroused intense criticism from conservatives in the church who were oblivious to the way their forbears had used non-Labor political parties. Clearly, the CSOM appealed to only a minority of Anglicans.

More radical than the CSOM was Bishop Burgmann. He developed close links with the Labor Government, establishing a friendship with Evatt who regarded this bishop as fighting a lonely battle on behalf of social reform. Burgmann strongly supported the 1944 referendum and agreed with Bishop Moyes of the CSOM about the way prejudice and misinformation had defeated it. But Burgmann went further after its defeat in supporting the left wing Labor view that the government should seek to control private capitalism.

By contrast, the majority of Burgmann's Anglican colleagues concentrated much more on evangelical witness and concern about symptoms of moral decline during the war. Sydney's conservative evangelical Archbishop, Howard Mowll, gave hesitant support to the CSOM. He devoted major energy to evangelisation campaigns and to organising chaplains and support services for the armed forces. But Sydney's churches were unable to protect the already much breached Sabbatarian Sunday, given a boost by the Curtin government's regulation issued in April 1942 empowering State Premiers to permit Sunday entertainment for the armed services. The Catholic-influenced New South Wales Labor Government allowed concerts, one cinema and one theatre to open on Sundays for entertaining the Australian and hordes of American troops in Sydney.

The Country Party Government in Victoria, ruled by the canny and frugal Presbyterian Albert Dunstan, bowed to church pressure by banning 'commercialism' on Sundays. His strategy was to allow cinemas to open on Sundays only if they charged half price which none was willing to do. An occasional free concert enlivened dull Melbourne Sunday afternoons.

South Australian Methodists participated readily in five national days of prayer in the first two years of the war. The first one on 8 September 1939 saw 33000 people congregate on Adelaide oval. Methodist leaders rejoiced that church services were much fuller in the early years of the war, but then were concerned that numbers dropped as the war progressed. The South Australian Methodist leadership still had a fixation about the twin evils of drinking and gambling. This campaign did achieve the closure of betting shops and a temporary suspension of horse racing. But temperance pressure made no progress, and the church was unable to hold the sabbatarian line, breached heavily with the influx of American troops in 1942 and the opening of Sunday entertainments for them. Wartime Methodist conferences from 1943 were willing to pass, though with heated debate, resolutions favouring a national insurance plan, a comprehensive health scheme, and a basic wage high enough for adequate personal development. These were revolutionary motions compared with past practice. They reflected the growing influence of the social gospel during the 1930s, enriching the radical strain of the Primitive Methodist past. But the resolutions probably did not reflect the majority view of lay Methodist church members.

Most shocking for Catholic and Protestant clergy during the war was the loosening of sexual morality. This was influenced by the uncertainties for the future, new freedoms for the many women entering the workforce for the first time, and the influx of big-spending Americans. There was talk of hordes of girls roaming streets and of rampant public love-making under the cover of night time blackouts. Catholics blamed bitterly the issuing of free contraceptives to Australian troops. The Labor Federal Government responded by banning the advertising of contraceptives. Mannix reacted by ordering the introduction of sex education into Catholic schools. He confessed that 'all of us are too puritanical in matters of sex', a view rather shocking to the many morally conservative Catholics.[6] Evidence of the moral decline was an increase in venereal disease cases, though not as much as alarmists suggested. There was also a threefold increase from 1937 to 1947 in the divorce rate in Australia.[7]

The Post-war Christian order

Despite concerns about the moral order, the Second World War had arrested the previous religious decline. It is true that in a Gallup poll in 1950, when respondents were asked if they attended church every week, only 6% of Anglicans said 'yes' plus 11% of Presbyterians and 19% of Methodists. Catholics were the exception with 62% answering in the affirmative. The total weekly attendance rate was 23%, nearly half the effective adult weekly attendance in New South Wales in 1890. However, the decline in Protestant church attachment at this stage was more in weekly attendance at church services than in church attendance overall. Adding figures for respondents who said they went to church at least once a month, which is the modern day sociological definition of 'regular' church attendance, the total rose to 47% of all respondents with a healthy Anglican increase to 34%, Presbyterians to 38%, Methodists to 46% and Catholics to 76%. The greater irregularity of attendance reflected the much wider weekend entertainment available in 1950 compared with 1890 as well as a diminution of religious fervour.[8]

Furthermore, of the church-attendance poll, only 24% of respondents said they never went to church, which probably was the late nineteenth-century actuality. Even if the 1950 statistic was biased in terms of what respondents were willing to admit to interviewers, that fact would indicate the still pervasive nature of the Christian presence in Australia. In the 1947 census, people declaring no religion or not answering that question had grown significantly, but only to 11.6%, compared with 2.7% in 1891. However, the big change in that category had occurred during the 1920s and early 1930s. In the previous census in 1933, 13% of people said they had no religion or did not answer the question. Also in 1947 only 0.3% of people confessed they followed no religion at all, compared with 0.4% who made that admission in 1921. So during the uncertainties of the depression and the war years people did not abandon their ultimate belief in God. Consequently, 87.8% of non-Aboriginal Australians declared they were Christian in 1947. The 0.4% who were Jews were the only other statistically significant religious sect. The only other census-enumerated non-Christian people were 2074 Muslims and 926 Buddhists, whose very small number reflected the secularisation and Christianisation of the Australian Chinese community.

The Muslims were mainly descendants of the 'Afghan' camel drivers, who came from the Pakistan region of British India as well as from Afghanistan. They had been crucial in the exploration of the desert regions of Australia and for managing a widespread network of camel transport across Central Australia, which in the 1920s was largely taken over by motor vehicles. In the mid-1950s, a former camel train headquarters, Marree, in northern South Australia, was still identifiably an 'Afghan' town. The Muslims lived in galvanised iron sheeting houses, with a tin mosque, segregated on one side from the shanties of Aborigines and on the other side from the few Europeans, who looked down on both races but respected the Afghans more. Most of the Afghans in that town were too poor to provide secondary education for their children—only available in distant Port Augusta. The relative poverty of the Muslim community in Australia was indicated by the fact that, in 1933, 74% of Muslim male breadwinners earned less than £52 per year, twice the national average.[9] There was significant intermarriage between Afghans and Aborigines.

Living in Adelaide on and off during the 1950s was a well-educated and cultured Muslim immigrant from Afghanistan, Mahamet Allum. He had faced hostility from the city's doctors in the 1930s when he established a herbalist business. But he gained fame as a healer of ailments and for his ready distribution of money to victims of the depression. At the age of eighty-one, he married an eighteen-year-old former patient and his assistant, after she had converted to Islam. He published pamphlets in which he expressed sadness at the prejudice and ignorance among Christian Australians about Islam and pleading for tolerance for all faiths living in 'God's earth'.[10]

A young Methodist minister in Adelaide discovered the widely pervasive belief in God when in 1953 he conducted a door-knock in one of the burgeoning new housing areas of the city. Hardly anybody he met denied the existence of God and almost all claimed membership of one or other Christian denomination. Most of the Protestants did not attend church services, with a common excuse that it was 'a thing that just wasn't done in this generation'.[11] However, they were almost unanimous in saying that the church was important for the community, and that their children should be baptised and sent to Sunday school to learn moral values.

Also the fall in church attendance tended to occur most in working class suburbs and among the working class dispersed to new housing areas. In Richmond, St Stephens Presbyterian Church was slowly dying to the point of closing its doors in 1965. The suburb's men preferred to spend Sunday mornings drinking at Ma Titut's Sunday Morning Club in South Richmond. One reason for the Protestant decline was the changing demographic pattern of the suburb with Australian-born residents moving out and some of the flood of post-war immigrants moving in. But the working class Protestants going to housing commission zones in new suburbs also left behind their former habits of church attendance.*

However, in the newer middle class suburbs of Melbourne, churches were overflowing. At the North Balwyn Methodist Church, one of its members in the 1950s said later: 'We flocked to that church. We were all the same. Our husbands were ex-servicemen and we came to build peace. We had ideals and we came to bring our children up in the church'.[12] In the 1950s, in this Melbourne 'Bible Belt', integrating children into the life of the church was seen as a moral and social necessity.

---

* That was certainly my experience. At the beginning of the 1950s, at the Hughesdale state school in southeast suburban Melbourne, I met boys from the nearby new housing commission homes who had migrated from working class suburbs such as Collingwood and Richmond. They introduced me to a new and bewilderingly different irreligious outlook from that of my Methodist middle class home, with their hard swearing and smutty jokes. Certainly, none of them went to the Oakleigh Methodist Church and Sunday school which I attended every week.

In the 1950s Protestant churches, especially Methodists, put much effort into countering their perception of declining attendance and moral decay. In Adelaide, Methodist women's groups were shocked when they heard from a police detective in 1956 about nude dancing at bodgie and widgie orgies on Saturday nights and that none of the 'uncontrolled' children appearing in the Juvenile Court had received any religious instruction. The answer was clear. It was expressed in a poster prepared in 1952 by the Australian Council of the World Council of Churches (ACWCC) depicting children entering a Sunday school with the slogan: 'Sunday School—where Good Citizenship Begins'.[13] The Australian Methodist Church responded with a Mission to the Nation, from 1953 to 1957, led by Alan Walker, a charismatic Sydney-based Methodist minister. He was different from previous evangelists who mostly came from the United States to sweep through Australia. He reflected the spreading influence of the social gospel by mixing his evangelistic message with declarations that the church should be involved in social justice problems. In the first year of the mission he attracted enormous crowds: 45 000 people came to his eight-day mission in the Brisbane City Hall, which climaxed with a march of 6000 people through Brisbane's streets. In subsequent years attendances were smaller.

The social gospel of Methodist campaigns in the 1950s was still mixed with moral concerns. For example, in 1958, the politically radical Rex Mathias recruited Frank Hartley, the socialist superintendent of the Prahran Methodist Mission, and Aboriginal Pastor Doug Nicholls of the Church of Christ, to speak on the theme 'Let's Talk Gambling Out' in the town hall of the Melbourne working-class suburb of Prahran.* The attendance of 400 reported in the press was an exaggeration, and many in the audience were grey-haired ladies, who were the last people needing to be convinced of the evils of gambling. In 1959, Methodist and other Protestant churches were enthused and re-energised by the first visit to Australia of the traditional American evangelist, Billy Graham, who played emotionally on the guilt feelings of thousands of his listeners who came forward to pledge their lives to Christ and who were organised back into their churches by campaign counsellors. While evidence suggests that he did not make many new Christians, he was powerful enough to stem tides of backsliding among previous middle class church attenders.

---

* As a school student at the time, I was also recruited to speak.

These evangelistic campaigns and the continued family-oriented appeal of the churches in the 1950s helped to maintain the level of Christian belief and practice. In 1961, the 62158 additional children since 1951 in Methodist Sunday Schools represented a 40% increase, which was significantly better than the growth rate of the Australian population. This was in marked contrast to England, where the number of Methodist Sunday School scholars declined by 38% in the same period. In a 1961 Gallup poll, Australians attending church 'weekly' had increased to 27%, and the 25% 'never' going to church remained close to the 1950s level. The monthly attendance rate was 44%, three percentage points less than in 1950, which would have mostly reflected a decline in Catholic church weekly attendance to 54%. This was an 8% fall since 1950, which was confirmed by three opinion polls in 1960–61. This downturn indicates that forces of secularisation and materialism which had produced earlier Protestant decline were now biting into the Australian Catholic church. Methodists showed the benefit of their evangelistic activities in the 1950s by raising their weekly attendance to 33%, now well ahead of the 14% of Presbyterians and 13% of Anglicans.[14]

The retention of past church going patterns helped perpetuate a continued social gulf between Catholics and Protestants. Australian children grew up in separate religious communities as Edmund Campion has revealed in his study of the life-formation of Catholics in Sydney.*[15] The Protestant student world was also one of continued puritan moral values. For example, in the late 1950s at a youth camp of the Darling Road Methodist Church of the Melbourne middle class suburb of East Malvern, when one of the boys was found in a girl's room, both were banished into the late night air by the outraged guest house owner.

Assisting the retention of Protestant church-going patterns in Australia was the persistence of Christian moral values at the national level.

* In my own Melbourne Methodist family there were two undesirable classes of Australians, Catholics and Labor voters, and they were identified together. As a young boy, I travelled to my state school on one side of a street and sang ditties, such as 'Dirty Catholic frogs sitting on logs', at Catholic kids on the other side. They replied in kind. My mother was horrified when in 1958 I started going out with a Catholic girlfriend, who was the first Catholic I had met, apart from Xavier College opponents on athletic tracks and football fields.

On Remembrance Day, 11 November 1951, the leaders of the Roman Catholic, Anglican, Presbyterian and Methodist churches and the ACWCC issued a 'Call to the People of Australia' signed also by the Chief Justices of every Australian State, read by the Chairman of the Australian Broadcasting Commission (ABC) immediately after the 7 p.m. news, carried by all but two commercial radio stations and printed in every daily newspaper on the next day. It emphasised the threat of international Communism to Australia; it highlighted the dangers of 'moral and intellectual apathy'; and it called for a 'restoration of the moral order from which alone true social order can derive'.[16]

Protestant politics in the 1950s

Presiding over that moral order was the federal Liberal Party Government, which was elected in 1949. Although its leader, Robert Menzies, had long abandoned the staunch Methodist faith of his childhood and only occasionally attended a Presbyterian church, befitting his later-life emphasis on his Scottish name, he sought to preserve Christian moral values. In his first Cabinet there was a mixture of both church-attenders and non-practising Protestants such as External Affairs Minister Richard Casey and the Minister for Home and Territories, Paul Hasluck. Hasluck had been raised strictly in the Salvation Army faith and turned away as a teenager, but it gave him a firm sense of public duty and social responsibility. Only two were Catholics. One of them was a former Fabian socialist, Senator Enid Lyons, the ex-Prime Minister's wife who had converted from her active Methodism to the Catholic faith of her husband. All Menzies' Ministers subscribed to the importance of Christianity as buttressing the social order. Menzies' political ideology, which he had expounded to radio audiences during the war under the theme of 'The Forgotten People', espoused a non-doctrinal Protestant ideology. It emphasised the value of the home, of moral values and of individual thrift. It was exemplified in his statement that: 'Human nature is at its greatest when it combines dependence upon God with independence of man'.[17] Part of this ideology and of the skilful politics of the Menzies Government was a stress on the threat of atheistic and tyrannical Communism, which it claimed had infected the Labor Party.

A clear majority of Protestants identified with the anti-socialism and anti-Communism of the Menzies Government. Opinion polls during the 1950s showed an average of three of every five Anglicans, Presbyterians and Methodists supporting non-Labor parties.* When in 1951 Menzies tried to exploit the Cold War hysteria, which had increased during the Korean War, with a constitutional referendum to ban the Communist Party, most Protestant church people supported it. An opinion poll estimated from 59% to 61% of Methodists, Anglicans and Presbyterians in favour, with the Catholic vote evenly split, though the actual vote was probably different given the defeat of the referendum.[18] Bishops Moyes and Burgmann were two vocal opponents who suffered much criticism from fellow Anglicans.

The anti-Communist climate in the Anglican church was pervasive. When in 1958 a new headmistress from England, Edith Mountain, arrived at the Melbourne Church of England Girls Grammar school and started overthrowing the school's liberal traditions, fifteen, teachers offered their resignations. But Ms Mountain was strongly supported by Archbishop Frank Woods, by the school council, and by parents who had been waiting for a chance to eradicate dangerous leftist tendencies from the school. The common undercurrent in this closing of conservative church ranks was a deep fear of Communism, even in cases where no such threat existed.

Political conservatism was also still the hallmark of other Protestant churches. In Canberra during the 1950s and well after, Presbyterian minister Hector Harrison was very careful not to reveal to his congregation that he voted Labor. In Victoria young radical Presbyterian ministers faced difficulty in finding parish settlements. There was strong opposition to the minority of Methodist clergy radicals who dissented from anti-Communist orthodoxy. Frank Hartley was one of them. In 1950 he was a founding member of the Australian Peace Council, which called for the banning of the atomic bomb, and which included some other clergy, such as the Presbyterian Alf Dickie, ASCM members, and secular socialists such as the Tasmanian Labor Senator Bill

* My first political memory was when, during the 1949 federal election campaign, my regular Methodist church-attending father gave me anti-Labor leaflets to drop into letter boxes on my way to school.

Morrow. For engaging in peace activities during the Korean War and afterwards, Hartley was branded as pro-Communist by many members of the Victorian Methodist Church.*

Catholics, Communism and trade unions

The Catholic church also was a strong supporter of post-war anti-Communist campaigns. In 1945 the Australian Catholic bishops agreed to combine the Movement with a clergy-managed similar organisation in Sydney into a national CSSM, supported financially by an Episcopal Committee, which was also responsible for its adherence to principles of Catholic faith. Santamaria was the new CSSM's Liaison Officer but in reality its head, and it was still under lay direction. Condemning the traditional view that the world could be reformed by individual acts of charity, Santamaria aimed 'at the creation of a Christian social order by means of large scale action in the social, economic, political and cultural spheres'.[19] While it had a much broader agenda for a Christian Australia, especially the regeneration of rural life, the new Movement concentrated on a crusade to defeat Communism in the trade unions.

The threat of Communism grew during the war. Germany's attack on the Soviet Union in June 1941 gave the Communists new respectability. The ban on the party was lifted by the Labor Government, and its renewed ability to campaign openly in unions was rewarded with a Communist majority at the Australian Council of Trade Unions (ACTU) Congress in Sydney in 1945. Communists also were involved, though not exclusively, in provoking a rash of wildcat strikes in 1945. Influential members of the Labor Party decided it was time to abandon the traditional Labor policy of non-interference in union affairs. The New South Wales party led the change at its 1945 annual conference. This conference authorised the setting up of Industrial Groups consisting of Labor Party members in workplaces to organise Labor candidates in union elections in order to defeat Communists.

Therefore, the CSSM had Labor Party supporters in its struggle against Communism in trade unions. Not all of them were Catholics

* But in 1958, at Methodism's elite Melbourne boys' school, Wesley College, I was taught the virtues of socialism by a social studies teacher which kick-started my leftward journey from the political conservativeness of my Methodist home.

however. One of Santamaria's major allies was the Protestant secretary of the Melbourne Trades Hall Council, Vic Stout. The Short family, whose son Laurie led the contest in the FIA, was Irish, but his father was Anglican Church of Ireland, and his mother was raised as a Presbyterian. Laurie Short was a Trotskyite critic of communism before becoming disillusioned with Marxism. The Labor Party Industrial Groups and the Movement provided a crucial organisational framework by borrowing the Communist method of forming cell groups which had regular meetings to plan strategies for union meetings and elections. Catholic priests cooperated by providing names of Catholic workers. When added to union opposition to Communist strike tactics, especially a coal strike in 1949 which crippled many industries, and the growing threat of international Communism, the Groups and the Movement, which had become closely identified together, gained major victories against Communist union leadership. They gave Laurie Short the means to win control of the FIA. They also succeeded in restoring an anti-Communist majority in the ACTU which was valuable for the defeat of the Mining Federation's coal strike by Ben Chifley's federal Labor Government. Jack Ferguson, a Catholic supporter of Industrial Groups in the Communist-led Australian Railways Union, led a New South Wales revolt against the national union's support for the coal strike, which saw railway workers in that State moving coal mined by strike-breaking troops.

Catholics and the Labor Party split

The success of the Industrial Groups sowed seeds of bitter opposition. An organised CSSM push, especially in Victoria, to ensure the election of dedicated anti-Communists to the Labor Party exacerbated this opposition. This push involved swamping party branches with Catholic members. Leo Fennessy, a Victorian Catholic politician, commented that Labor membership tickets were 'hawked' among Catholics attending mass in the inner Melbourne suburb of Brunswick. 'Many fellow parishioners of mine became party members', he said, 'but I never saw most of them at branch meetings'.[20] Their purpose was to influence ballots for party candidates. Consequently, of the nine new federal Labor Members of the House of Representatives elected in Victoria in 1949, seven were Catholics—all supporters of the Industrial Groups.

Concern about outside influences dominating the party was aggravated by the extension of Movement influence into non-Communist unions, especially the Transport Workers' Union. Its New South Wales branch was controlled by the Catholic, Barney Platt, who benefited personally from high prices charged for serving the union's fleet of cars at a garage he owned secretly and who was involved in union ballot manipulation.[21] Using this information, the CSSM moved to oust Platt, who had ceased supporting the Industrial Groups. However, the Catholic Coadjutor Bishop of Sydney, James Carroll, opposed the move because Platt was a good Catholic anti-Communist. Platt responded with a campaign accusing the Movement of targeting Labor men instead of Communists and was assisted by Tom Dougherty, the general secretary of the AWU. They formed the Combined Australian Labor Party Unions Steering Committee. Its aim was to oppose the trade union influence of Industrial Groups.

The Labor Party's federal leader, Herbert Evatt, now had a union base for launching a campaign against the Movement. He had been concerned about the growing Catholic influence in the party, though this had not stopped him from asking Santamaria for suggestions for his policy speech in the 1954 election campaign. After his narrow failure to win that election, influenced by the dramatic use by the Menzies Government of a defecting Russian spy, Vladimir Petrov, to cast false aspersions about Evatt's commitment to anti-Communism, the Labor leader's normal paranoia about personal enemies heightened. He announced on 5 October 1954: 'In the election, one factor told heavily against us—the attitude of a small minority group of members, located particularly in the State of Victoria, which has, since 1949, become increasingly disloyal to the Labor Movement and the Labor leadership'. This cabal, he charged, was 'largely directed from outside' the party; and he named, 'as their organ', the Melbourne-based CSSM journal, *News Weekly*, which had been banned by the party's federal executive for supporting Menzies' Communist Party referendum, and which was the mouthpiece of Santamaria.[22] Evatt had no good evidence to support this accusation about interference in the election campaign, although he had plenty of information about the Movement's influence in unions and the party. Whatever the justification, the statement was like a spark in a gunpowder factory.

The long-lasting tensions between right wing Catholics and others in the Labor Party going back to the early days of disputes about socialism, agitated most recently with differences about the anti-communism referendum, now exploded. The fall-out was greatest in Victoria. The refusal of Victoria's Movement-dominated Labor executive to bow to federal intervention, in an atmosphere of sectarianism and bitter recrimination, resulted in a stand-off between two rival sets of Victorian delegates to the national party's conference in Hobart in March 1955. Religion was not the only line of division on the question of which delegation would be admitted. While two-thirds of the seventeen 'pro-groupers' were Catholics, so too were a third of their nineteen opponents, such as Senator Patrick Kennelly of Victoria. The subsequent showdown in Victoria resulted in expulsions from the Labor Party. Seventeen State parliamentarians and seven members of the House of Representatives, six of whom had been new Catholic members elected in 1949 were expelled. The other federal parliamentarian expelled was Robert Joshua, an Anglican whose wife and six children were Catholic and who was a convenient token Protestant for the new Australian Labor Party (Anti-Communist), soon renamed the Democratic Labor Party (DLP).

The most immediate consequence was a vote by the expelled State members in favour of a Liberal Party vote of no confidence which brought down the Victorian Labor Government led by the Protestant John Cain. Subsequently, that branch of the Labor Party was excluded from office until his son led it to power again in 1982. The bitterness of the split in Victoria, which divided families as well as Catholic parishes, was as great as the savagery of the party split in 1916.

Queensland also saw a major Labor Party division. The Catholic Premiers, Ned Hanlon until his death in 1952 and then Vince Gair, supported the Industrial Groups. This support was alienating the AWU, exacerbated by personal enmity between Gair and the union's state president, Joe Bukowski, going back to their common Catholic childhood in Rockhampton. Also, the Industrial Groups in Queensland did not make the same inroads into unions as in Victoria. They were not able to unseat the Communist secretaries of the TLC mainly because the Catholic octogenarian Archbishop Duhig had shifted his attention to the federal government. He had placed his faith in Menzies, who had hinted that his party might be willing to grant the long sought state aid for Catholic schools. In the 1949 federal election campaign Duhig publicly announced his disenchantment with the way Labor had been seduced by socialism. Despite this, he remained friendly with the Hanlon and Gair State Labor Governments—two-thirds of their Ministers were

Catholics. But Duhig had paid no attention to the progress of the Industrial Groups. After their condemnation by Evatt in 1954, they came under increasing attack from an unholy alliance between the AWU and the Communist controlled TLC. After Premier Gair's refusal to act on a state party executive approval of three weeks' annual leave for workers, an alliance of the AWU, the TLC and anti-group parliamentary members moved against him. In April 1957 the executive expelled the Premier.

The consequent split arising from this action ran down the middle of the parliamentary party. Gair formed a Queensland Labor Party (QLP), which had twenty-five of the forty-nine Labor members of parliament, including all but one of Gair's Cabinet, which continued to govern. But the Labor remnant joined with the opposition to deny supply to the Government in June 1957. The party split resulted in electoral defeat for both Labor parties. Labor remained in the political wilderness until 1989.

However, there was no major Labor Party split in other States in the struggle over Industrial Groups. The Catholic Labor Premier of Tasmania, Robert Cosgrove, had read the political wind and distanced himself from the Movement before Evatt pounced. The Protestant-led Labor Government in Western Australia was not influenced by the Movement and placed party unity at a premium, refusing to carpet its four delegates who had joined pro-groupers at the Hobart conference. The South Australian Labor opposition was also firmly controlled by anti-groupers, who in 1951 had withdrawn State party authorisation from the Industrial Groups. This Labor party was supported by the Catholic Archbishop Beovich and most of his parish priests.

New South Wales, with the biggest Catholic population-minority, was a potential trouble spot. However, Cardinal Gilroy and Bishop Carroll had become alienated by the intervention of the Industrial Groups, not only into the Transport Workers Union, but also into other non-Communist unions. They were deeply concerned about the health of the Labor Party with which Catholics had enjoyed such a long and close relationship. They moved to control the Movement in their diocese, where there had been previous clerical supervision of lay movements. Furthermore, the divisions in New South Wales Labor in the 1930s and early 1940s encouraged the commitment of many of its parliamentary members to sink differences of opinion about the Industrial Groups. However, there was still some internal wrangling, and a federal party executive intervention resulted in a Catholic rump being expelled from the Labor Party. This rump formed a DLP in New South Wales.

The triumph of the anti-groupers in New South Wales led to the federal Labor Party withdrawing its recognition of the Industrial Groups. This brought a quick response in April 1955 from the Catholic bishops, who issued a joint pastoral letter condemning Communism and criticising Labor's ostracism of the Groups. But the Sydney diocese's subsequent move to control the Movement achieved majority episcopal support. The CSSM responded in 1957 by reorganising itself into the National Civic Council (NCC) with no formal links with the Catholic Church.

Voting for the DLP was one way for Catholics to punish Labor. By the November 1958 federal election, this new party had expanded from Victoria into all the other Australian States, except for Queensland, where Gair was leading the QLP. However, in that election there was no uniform support for the new Catholic Centre Party, as some were calling it. Hostility from the Catholic hierarchy in South Australia and New South Wales reduced the DLP proportion of their total vote to 6.1% and 5.7% respectively. However, strong clergy support in Western Australia and Victoria influenced higher respective DLP votes of 10.5% and 14.8%. But, even in Santamaria's home State of Victoria, the vote fell well below the Catholic proportion of 23% of the Victorian population in 1954, which under the impact of immigration from continental Europe rose to 26% by 1961. More than a third of Victorian Catholics therefore voted for other parties, including the Labor Party, which still contained some devout Catholics such as Kennelly and the deputy leader of the federal party, Arthur Calwell. In New South Wales, with the lowest national DLP vote, the Catholic proportion of the population was 25% in 1954. There the hierarchical opposition to the DLP resulted in less than a quarter of the State's Catholics voting for that party.[23]

The DLP did, however, achieve its major aim. Its preferences, which flowed strongly to the Liberal and Country Parties (LCP), assisted their victory. In 1958 the non-Labor government was able to retain office with 46.5% of the formal vote; and the DLP was able to assist in the preservation of non-Labor federal governments until 1972. It had seduced significant Catholic support from the Labor Party, as measured by the Gallup poll fall in the proportion of Catholics intending to vote Labor from 73% in 1949 to 52% in 1958.[24]

Continued paternalism and new policies for Aborigines

The nation's Aboriginal population had no role in the political dramas of the 1950s because they were still stateless people. The pre-war Christian paternalistic approach to them was threatened due to the effects of the Second World War. Many Christian missions in the Northern Territory were isolated as a part of federal government policy under the Elkin-influenced new order, where Aborigines would be separated from non-Aboriginal society to slowly catch up with European culture. The missions themselves had contributed to this isolation as sources of food for Aborigines.

From 1940 that isolation broke down with the building of airstrips and the influx of white airmen and soldiers after the outbreak of war against Japan. Mission Aborigines were used as labourers, and the white Australians from the south were a source of attraction to them. Many servicemen came from regions where there were no Aborigines and were pleasantly surprised to see virile Aboriginal people who did not conform to the derelict stereotype common in Australian society. Not having absorbed the racism of the north, many of the newcomers treated Aborigines with an egalitarianism that shocked missionaries. A Catholic missionary at the Drysdale River mission in northern Western Australia wrote in 1942 that the Aborigines were 'becoming very bold and insolent, abusing our kindness'.[25] The superintendent of the Presbyterian mission on Mornington Island was offended at soldiers allowing Aborigines to call them by their first names. The army also provided its Aboriginal employees with the same living conditions and other services as for white soldiers, with the exception of perpetuating the pre-war Aboriginal wage-rate of five shillings per week. But in some circumstances service pay rates for Aboriginal employees rose to as much as £2/5/- per week compared with the initial payment for white Australian militia soldiers of £2 per week. Missions withheld this money from their Aborigines. Arthur Ellemore, the supervisor of the Methodist Milingimbi Mission in the Northern Territory, explained: 'We would only be doing these primitive folk a disservice if we in any way flooded them with things they do not know how to handle or have any real need of'.[26]

After the war there was a new response to Aboriginal mission work in the Anglican ABM. Social justice ideas which had surfaced at the 1937 NMCA conference, and which were expressed during the war by the CSOM, helped the acceptance of a project proposed by a radical Anglican priest, Alfred Clint. Clint had grown up in poverty and was influenced in Sydney by the Christian socialism of John Hope before he joined the Bush Brotherhood and earned unpopularity during the 1930s among conservative Anglicans in western New South Wales for supporting workers' rights. After the war, he had responded to an invitation from the Bishop of New Guinea to develop indigenous cooperative trading enterprises there. Invalided back to Australia in 1951, he sold the idea of developing similar cooperatives among Aborigines to the ABM in the conviction that this was a non-exploitative and culturally appropriate approach to integrate indigenous people into European economies. In 1953, the ABM appointed Clint as Director of Cooperatives. He established cooperative ventures at the Lockhart River Mission in northern Queensland, on Moa Island in the Torres Strait, and at Cabbage Tree Island in northern New South Wales as well as a cooperative training college for Aborigines in Sydney. But by the end of the decade there were signs of impending failure with the declaration of bankruptcy of the Lockhart cooperative because of a collapse in the market for the trochus shell it sold.

Elkin also changed his attitude to Aborigines after the war. He had kept in close touch with their wartime experiences and was astounded to learn that they thrived under the cultural disruption of employment by the armed services as labourers and as soldiers. This upset his theory justifying the need to segregate Aborigines from white society. He realized that the new status, better living conditions and better food had benefited Aborigines. Characteristically, he jumped into action to propound his new theory in a pamphlet entitled *Citizenship for the Aborigines*. This called for implementing local self-government for Aborigines; outlawing the practice of substituting food and shelter for wages; and eventually admitting all Aborigines into full Australian citizenship. But the Labor Government was not interested. However, Elkin persisted, assisted by his status as *the* Australian expert on Aborigines, and by carefully planned non-confrontationist styles of lobbying.

Nevertheless, Elkin's influence was limited. It did help to improve education for cadets of the new Commonwealth Department of Aboriginal Affairs and for school teachers in the Northern Territory. But it did not lead to the expunging of racist laws from statute books or the granting of any land rights to Aborigines. He wielded less influence on hide-bound State government bureaucracies, except New South Wales, where he became Vice-Chairman of its Aborigines Welfare Board. His new view of Aboriginal capabilities had made him an assimilationist: policies to help Aborigines fit into European society. This policy position included the continued sanction of forcible removal of Aboriginal children from their parents into European foster homes and missions with no concern about the traumatic experiences suffered by children and, especially, their mothers. He also still remained convinced that there were racial, including intellectual, differences between Europeans and Aborigines. His self-righteousness and paternalistic style were blinding him to emerging radical cries from Aborigines themselves and some white supporters for true racial justice.

Assimilation was the new buzz word for the Menzies Government. It was stung into action not only because of Elkin's pressure, but also because of United Nations criticism of Australia's continued mistreatment of Aborigines. But there was still an old-style paternalism about a new Northern Territory Welfare Ordinance which made full-blood Aborigines 'wards' of the State, subject to complete control by the Director of Welfare. This new ordinance was in line with mission policy since the early years of the century which had concentrated on gradually preparing Aborigines for eventual incorporation into European society. The Anglican CMS, influenced by Elkin and the Methodist Mission Board, had become more open to the indigenous culture and languages of Aborigines, while still working for their ultimate assimilation into white Australia. Nor could racist attitudes on mission stations be changed overnight. Also portending a new culture clash between Aborigines and white Australians was an agreement in 1958 between the Methodist Mission Board and the Northern Territory Administration for the granting of a mining lease on mission property. No Aborigines were consulted in this arrangement.

Portents of change in Christian influence

By the end of the 1950s there were signs that the plateau in the decline of influence of Protestant Christianity in Australia was about to descend into a new valley of secularism. In 1954 in New South Wales, the State with the most tenuous Protestant influence, a strong campaign by the Methodist and other Protestant churches for a 'no' vote in a referendum to end six o'clock hotel closing in favour of 10 p.m. narrowly failed. Two years later, the well-entrenched State Labor Government legalised poker machines in clubs, despite a campaign from Protestant churches that they were 'morally vicious' and that the temptation they would offer would lead to family destitution.[27] The Methodist Church protested in vain when in 1958 the Sydney Rugby League started playing Sunday matches. In Western Australia in 1954 the Labor Government legalised off-course betting, which did not stop it being re-elected two years later.

Also during the 1950s economic prosperity, the most corrosive agent in the erosion of Christian belief, was transforming Australian life. After the destitution of the Great Depression and the austerity of the Second World War and its aftermath, the 1950s opened up a new world of consumerism. There were new household products, ranging from Heinz baby food to laminex table tops, new sources of entertainment such as television and long-playing records; and new sources of mobility represented by the Holden motor car. These products could be purchased with real wage rises fueled by the Korean War-generated commodity price boom, or by means of hire purchase credit. The advertising industry went to ever greater lengths to stimulate the rush of Australians to acquire a new modern life style. This frenetic modernisation was providing new distractions and new confidence in human endeavour, whilst at the same time developing acquisitive materialism and selfishness which were antithical to self-giving faith in Jesus Christ or even belief in a supreme God. This was especially so for the previously high church-going middle classes. Working class people who enjoyed less of the consumer boom had long been largely alienated from Protestant churches. The evangelistic crusades of the 1950s were merely the erection of flood gates which in the 1960s would prove too weak to hold the onrushing tide of consumer-driven secularism.

Summary

During the Second World War and into the 1950s Christianity was marking time in its influence in Australia. Christian moral values were still upheld at the national level, especially by the Menzies Liberal Government. Churches had retained their hold on nearly half the Australian population—and many more of the middle class—in frequent worship attendance. Only Catholics experienced the symptoms of earlier Protestant decline. The Catholic and Protestant communities were still separated socially, but there was no renewed political sectarianism except within the Labor Party as it was torn asunder by the Catholic crusade against Communism. Protestants still clung to their conservative political and moral values. Changes in approaches to Aborigines were still influenced by paternalism. The change from a policy of separation to the new emphasis on assimilation was a continued Eurocentric approach.

CHAPTER SIX

THE MAKING OF POST-CHRISTIAN AUSTRALIA, *1961–1993*

In the 1960s attendance at Christian churches started to decline again. There also were other signs of diminishing Christian influence in the Australian community. This chapter discusses the extent of this decline and recent signs of a small religious upsurge. It also examines the rise of non-Christian faiths as a result of post-war immigration, and the development of new Christian attitudes and changing religious practices in the Aboriginal community.

The decline of Christian practice

In 1966 Hans Mol measured the beginnings of a new decline in Christian church attendance. His survey of 2607 carefully selected adults in New South Wales, Victoria and Tasmania revealed that 27% attended church 'nearly always', that is three times per month or more, and 39% at least once per month. The monthly rate was five percentage points less than that of the 1961 Gallup Poll. The 'nearly always rate' was the same as weekly attendance in 1961. But Catholic attendance showed a 5% improvement to 60%, whereas Methodists had fallen from 33% to 27%, Presbyterians three percentage points to 16% and Anglicans two points to 11%. This survey's results matched contemporary patterns of church attendance in New Zealand and England. But in the United States, where Christianity has always had a higher profile, beginning with the religious nature of much of its early European settlement, over a third of Methodists and Episcopalians and more than two-thirds of Catholics and Presbyterians attended church at least once a week.[1]

The 1966 study went deeper than any previous surveys of religious beliefs in Australia. It revealed that women were more regular church attenders, but only by a factor of seven women for every six men among Methodists and Catholics and for every five less frequent church-attending male Anglicans and Presbyterians. A surprising result was that young adults, aged twenty to twenty-four, had virtually the same monthly rate of church attendance as each of the other age groups. But less than half as many young adults (22%) prayed daily as did those over sixty years of age (46%). Social mobility of Catholics by this stage had largely closed the previous class gap. The Australian Survey project in the following year indicated a big disparity in working class monthly church goers: 47% of Catholics and 16% of Protestants. Mol also divided his group into believers and secularists who had no significant church attendance and at best a wavering faith in God. The secularists outnumbered the believers by 43% to 42%.[2]

By 1983, as revealed in the Australian Values Study Survey, monthly church attendance had declined from 47% in 1950 to 27%. Catholics had participated in this decline to 46% and Anglicans to 16%. The proportion of monthly worshippers had dropped to 23% for Presbyterians and the Uniting Church (formed in 1977 and incorporating almost all Methodists, over 90% of Congregationalists and about two-thirds of the Presbyterians). By contrast, the smaller numbers of Baptists, Lutherans and other fundamentalist and evangelical religious sects had a monthly attendance rate of 56%.[3]

Significantly, the number of people in the 1983 survey who never went to church had risen from 24% in 1950 to 37%. Adding the 11% who said they attended worship services less often than once a year, the group not going to church had reached nearly half of this sample of Australians and 41% said they were not 'religious', though only 5% were willing to identify themselves as 'atheist'. The 1986 census further revealed the growing trend of people willing to describe themselves as having no religion. That proportion had reached 13%, compared with 0.4% in 1961, which was similar to the proportion in the previous twentieth century censuses. Along with people who did not reply to the religious question in 1986 or described their response inadequately, 23% of Australians did not identify themselves as 'religious'.

The decline in Christian practice and significance was studied by Kenneth Dempsey in a Victorian country 'smalltown' of 2700 people who were serving another 1050 people in a farming community. The Anglican and Uniting Churches, which comprised two-thirds of the population, had congregations in 1990 of half their size in 1970. Less than 10% of the community's Protestants would be in church on a given Sunday. A portent for the future was the imbalance of elderly people at worship services. There was also concern in the town's Catholic Church about attendances at mass which had declined by a quarter in the previous two decades. Religious identity in this small community was evaporating. Only 9% of people surveyed made any reference to religion when discussing their friendship patterns. People had difficulty in recognising the names of church groups and generally viewed the churches as anachronistic 'private clubs'.[4]

Diminishing public Christianity

Indeed, by the 1980s, compared with the 1950s, the influence of Christianity and Christian values had declined greatly in the Australian community. At the national level, the Labor Government elected in 1983 had members who were practising Christians, such as the Victorian Uniting Church minister Brian Howe and the devout Catholic Tasmanian Senator Michael Tate. The Prime Minister, 'Bob' Hawke, was the son of a Congregationalist minister but an avowed agnostic. The second most important member of the Hawke ministry, Treasurer Paul Keating, was a Catholic who became Prime Minister in 1992. The emphases of the Hawke and Keating governments, in order of priority, have been on community consensus, economic rationalism, Australian nationalism and social justice. There was no specific religious content in these policies but not all symbols of Christianity have been removed. In 1993 prayers were still said in the Federal Parliament. But the Bible was no longer required in the swearing of oaths and few Labor politicians attended the annual church service for the opening of the parliamentary year organised by the minority Parliamentary Christian Fellowship.

More politicians of the opposition Liberal and National Parties (LNP) went to parliamentary worship services, such as one of the Liberal leaders of the 1980s, Andrew Peacock, who was an Anglican.

Politicians from these parties still espoused Menzies-style moral values, but there was little of the social welfare content of the Menzies era in their policies. Instead there was a growing emphasis on economic rationalism, devoid of social justice concerns. This 'new right' philosophy appealed to self-centered individualism and was damned as 'the cult of selfishness' by the Australian historian, Hugh Stretton.[5]

The collapse of the Protestant moral order

Labor and some Liberal State governments continued to dismantle the restraints of Protestant moral control. In South Australia, after the overthrow of the long-serving Liberal Country League Government in 1965, there were two Labor governments, mostly under the leadership of the flamboyant Don Dunstan. Until 1972 Dunstan was a lay representative on the synod of the Anglican diocese of Adelaide. But he was a secular-minded product of the post-war development of liberalism and social justice within mainstream churches. He and his Labor and Liberal predecessors presided over the ending of six o'clock hotel trading, the extension of liquor licences, the implementation of legalised off-course betting and a State lottery, liberalisation of abortion laws and the decriminalisation of homosexuality. Conservative Christians viewed his government as the worst example of secular humanism, introducing a regime of 'moral permissiveness'. In 1973 a group of evangelicals decided to 'make a stand against moral decline' by forming the Festival of Light in Adelaide. This was a national conservative evangelical pressure group to campaign for the restoration of 'Christian standards of behaviour in law and family life'.[6]

A problem for conservative South Australian Christians was that the past standard-bearer of moral reform in their State, the Methodist Church, was no longer as enthusiastic or united in this cause. In 1966, with the allegiance of 21% of the population, Methodism was second only to the Anglican church in size and political influence in South Australia. However, by then some of its younger clergy had been influenced by radical Christian thought, an extension of the social gospel of the past. 'Religionless' Christianity, exemplified by the influential book by the American author Harvey Cox, *The Secular City*, denounced the church role of moral guardian and emphasised instead faith in Jesus Christ. This 'secular' Christian belief identified moral codes with the Judaic law which Jesus overthrew.

However, secular Christianity was by no means a majority clerical view in South Australian Methodism. When in November 1965 the new Labor Government implemented a referendum on government promotion of lotteries, the Methodist Church organised a 'No Lottery' committee and, with the support of the Anglican Bishop of Adelaide and the leaders of the two Lutheran churches, ran a vigorous campaign for a 'no' vote. But 71% of South Australians voted 'yes'.

The cause for moral reform was lost and attitudes within the church had changed. The Methodist conference still voted during the early 1970s to oppose a casino in Adelaide and approved abstinence from alcohol as an ideal whilst recognising that many Methodists now drank alcohol and gambled. The conference supported the government's move to decriminalise homosexuality and refused to identify with the Festival of Light. The Anglican Archbishop, Keith Rayner, also supported lifting the ban on homosexuality. These changing attitudes towards moral order among South Australia's Methodists and other mainstream Christians gave the Dunstan Government a green light for some of its social reforms.

Similar problems with the Protestant moral order occurred in other States. In Victoria, when the Liberal Government proposed extending hotel hours from 6 p.m. to 10 p.m., Methodists who were gearing up to oppose this policy were shocked when their spokesman on social issues, the Rev. John Westerman, shifted his allegiance to support the move. The policy was implemented in February 1966 with minimal opposition.

Defending the moral order was left to conservatives of the Festival of Light and similar evangelical bodies. In New South Wales, the Uniting Church minister Fred Nile, a leader of the Festival of Light, was elected, with over 9% of the primary vote, to the New South Wales Legislative Council after the introduction of proportional representation. He was joined there later by his wife. The Niles operated in a more conservative religious environment in Sydney than in Adelaide and Melbourne. It was the home of the uniquely evangelical Anglican diocese of Sydney. Sydney was also the city in which the largest body of Presbyterians refused to join the Uniting Church and continued as an increasingly conservative Presbyterian Church. Sydney Methodists were more evangelical than their South-Australian or Victorian colleagues and formed one of the most conser-vative groups within the Uniting Church. Social justice ideas have also had less influence in the Sydney Catholic diocese than in Melbourne.

A major reason for this conservatism was the smaller influence of Christianity in a State which, from the beginning, had a large number of opponents of Christianity, and in which church attendance has always been less than in other States, especially Victoria and South Australia. Sydney Christians have had more of a siege mentality against hedonistic secularism, witnessed by the intensity of their moral reform programs in the earlier twentieth century. Many Sydney Methodists were disenchanted with the social justice content of Walker's mission to the nation in the 1950s. Secular Christianity of the 1960s took shallower root in Sydney's Protestant Churches than in the other states. Hence the greater popularity and influence of the Festival of Light and the need for more liberal Christians to organise their own ecumenical council in order to escape from the conservativeness of the New South Wales Council of Churches.

However, by the 1960s the political influence of evangelical Protestantism had long waned in New South Wales. In 1966, the new LCP Government repealed the *Sunday Observance Act*, allowing theatres and cinemas to open, and sporting events to charge admission. Neville Wran, the smooth-talking lawyer and Labor Premier from 1976, demonstrated his government's distance from Protestant moralism, and even from Labor values, by partially farming out to private enterprise the gambling game of Lotto, for the sole purpose of generating maximum revenue for the government from its percentage of profits. Also in December 1979 the Wran government had the temerity to legalise the opening of hotels on Sundays. In 1981 it increased its substantial parliamentary majority in a 'Wranslide' State election.

A sign of the collapse of the moral order was the abandonment of many censorship rules in Australia. By the 1990s this new freedom extended to the legal availability in the national capital of x-rated videos depicting sexual acts in comprehensive detail and protected by the minority Labor Government of the Australian Capital Territory (ACT). A contributing factor is that such pornography no longer excites the alarm of many mainline Christians in Canberra. Though they are not necessarily comfortable about its presence, their churches have mounted no campaign against it.

Another by-product of the decline of Christian influence was booming crime rates. By 1975 the rate of convictions for offences against the person in Australia, compared with 1935, had almost trebled. The rate of convictions for crimes against property had more than doubled. In the 1980s the decline in standards of probity in the Australian business world became a national scandal.

By the 1980s the state also had taken over social services that were previous domains of Christian churches. The dole for unemployed people during the 1930s depression had been a response to the inability of Christian and other charitable activities to cope with the unemployment disaster. The Labor Governments of the 1940s introduced the welfare state into Australia. Widows' pensions, family allowances, funeral benefits and wider unemployment provisions, along with Commonwealth funding for housing and health, were designed to provide 'a cradle to the grave' safety net for all non-Aboriginal Australians. The next Federal Labor Government (1972–75) greatly increased the government's social expenditure to ensure a basic minimum living standard for all, now including Aborigines. In a period of worsening unemployment and soaring inflation, the number of dependents on government social services doubled from 1971 to 1981, and there was a doubling of the proportion of gross domestic product devoted to social expenditure from 1960 to 1985.[7] Church hospitals, homes for children and the elderly and social service organisations were still an important sector of this social welfare network and some had high public credibility, such as the Salvation Army and the Anglican Brotherhood of St Laurence. However, Church bodies were subject to government funding and regulatory controls and played minor roles in comparison with the huge expansion of government services.

The divorce between Catholicism and Labor

The political power of the Catholic Church in Australian Labor parties was also disappearing. There were still Catholics in the Wran Government but they were a minority. The marriage between the Church and the New South Wales Labor Party, which had survived the Industrial Group-influenced divorce in Victoria and Queensland, foundered on the old issue of State aid. Seen as a reward for keeping Labor in office, the Church had to apply the pressure of public agitation to achieve State funding for schools that were struggling to cope with rapidly increasing community demands for secondary education. The campaign opened with a meeting in July 1962 of 500 Catholics in Goulburn, with episcopal support, which threatened to close Catholic schools if State aid were not granted, practically demonstrated with a temporary closure of Catholic schools in that provincial city. The State Labor conference saw the political writing on the wall, and in June 1963 agreed to government assistance 'in the provision of science laboratories and teaching facilities in all schools' if such needs existed. However, the post-split federal Labor executive, shorn of previous right wing Catholic strength, was determined to maintain the traditional anti-State aid policy. Influenced by its secretary, the powerful Western Australian, F. E. 'Joe' Chamberlain, it used its party authority to overturn the New South Wales conference policy. Chamberlain said confidently: 'We will pick up as many votes from Protestants against State aid as we will lose from Catholics who want it'.[8]

But Chamberlain was out of date. There was little political mileage left in Protestant anti-Catholicism. The evangelical New South Wales Council of Churches strongly opposed granting any advantages to Catholic schools. However, an opinion poll in 1964, concerning the Menzies Federal Governments acceptance, under pressure from the Catholic schools lobby and the DLP, of £6 million assistance for private school science blocks, showed 65% of respondents in favour. These included 59% of Anglicans, 56% of Presbyterians and 55% of Methodists. The Rev. Alan Dougan, moderator of New South Wales' Presbyterian Church, called for an end to sectarian prejudice and for Protestant schools to accept the aid. The political fall-out from Menzies' initiative was the withdrawal of Catholic support from the State Labor Party and its decisive defeat in the 1965 State election.

Australia's involvement in another war widened the split between the Catholic Church and the Labor Party. In April 1965, the Menzies Government announced the commitment of Australian troops to the Vietnam War. The Federal Labor Party, led by the devoutly Catholic Arthur Calwell, opposed this policy from the start. He objected especially to the conscription of one in four young Australian men for this purpose, introduced in the previous November. However, the traditional opposition to Communism encouraged Catholic Church support for Australian military intervention. Australia's participation was justified by 'anti-Communist rhetoric'. The United States had to be helped in its struggle against the perceived threat of Soviet and Chinese-backed North Vietnamese Communism spreading into South Vietnam. Catholic support for the war was reinforced by the financial aid granted by the Menzies Government to Catholic schools. In those schools anti-Communism was expressed with religious fervour, influencing many of their graduates to support the government's military assistance for American forces in Vietnam. One of them, Val Noone, explained: 'We were brought up to support the American intervention in Vietnam and to identify American foreign policy with our Catholic faith'.[9]

In Victoria, strong support for the Vietnam War came from Santamaria's NCC which was vigorously continuing the anti-Communist cause of the former Movement. Mannix's successor, Archbishop Justin Simmonds, wished to cut the linkage between church and politics. But he made no public statement and was elderly and ailing. The diocese was managed by disciples of Mannix, who maintained a staunch pro-Vietnam War line. The Victorian Catholic *Advocate*, which initially raised a question about the morality of the war, was silenced on the issue. Some Catholics dissented, such as Max Charlesworth, a philosophy lecturer at the University of Melbourne, who declared it an unjust war and identified correctly that China was not a staunch supporter of North Vietnam.

In Sydney there was also some Catholic dissent, for example by Paul Ormonde, an ABC radio journalist. But a group of Sydney lay people, who formed in 1967 a 'Catholics for Peace' group, received a frosty reception from Cardinal Gilroy. There was no Australian Catholic episcopal criticism of the war. The reaction was either approval for it or silence, while the NCC and the DLP whipped up strong Catholic support for the cause.

The consequent desertion of Catholic voters from Labor ranks was a major reason for a disastrous slide of the Labor vote at the next federal election in 1966. The vote fell by five percentage points to 40%. A Gallup poll on the eve of the election showed only 37% of Catholics who were interviewed intending to vote Labor, with another 9% who did not know how they would vote, compared with 52% of Catholics supporting Labor in 1958. Indeed, Mol's 1966 survey revealed only a quarter of Catholic regular church-attenders supporting Labor.[10]

The changed political situation in Australia was demonstrated with the election in 1972 of the first Federal Labor Government since 1949. The new Prime Minister, Gough Whitlam, was the non-church attending son of a Presbyterian elder. In Chifley's 1945–49 ministry there were sixteen Catholics, ten Protestants and one parlimentarian who was non-religious. In Whitlam's 1972–75 ministry there were seventeen Protestants, eleven Catholics, two Jews, and two with no religion. The Catholic proportion had dropped from 59% to 32%—much closer to the 27% of the Australian population who were Catholic in 1971. Another sign of the diminished liaison between the Catholic Church and Labor was Labor governments' agreement to abortion reform in the face of a vigorous Catholic-dominated 'Right to Life' movement determined to stop the process. The extent of that shift is measured by the ACT Labor Government's decision in 1993 to provide funding for an abortion clinic. In 1991 the ACT had a higher proportion of Catholics (31%) than any other Australian Territory or State.

There were other reasons for the divorce between Catholicism and Labor that were related to social mobility and anti-clericalism. David Kemp's survey of opinion poll data in 1974 concluded that only 30% of Catholics who had been middle class for two or more generations voted Labor, compared with 50% of those who had more recently moved into the middle class and 66% of those who had been working class for two or more generations. Even that working class support was less than the 73% of all Catholics who intended to vote Labor in 1949. By the time of the 1983 Australian Values Survey, when Labor won a handsome federal election victory, 54.5% of Catholics supported Labor, but so too did 52.7% of all respondents and 49.8% of Anglicans. Also, only 40% of the monthly church attenders of all denominations were pro-Labor.[11]

Radical versus conservative Christians

Protestant and Catholic conservatism came under more attack from Christian radicals during the 1960s and 1970s. A major breeding ground for Protestant radicalism was the ASCM in secondary schools and universities. It competed with the conservative Evangelical Union. For some of those in the ASCM it was a Christian life-line of escape from the moralistic Protestantism of their background without falling into the abyss of agnosticism or atheism as a result of exposure to the intellectual challenges and hedonistic temptations of student life. In Victoria the College Presbyterian Church, near the University of Melbourne, had a significant academic membership. Its predominant theology was the Christian gospel freed from moral law and directed to the service of humanity.*

However, young ministers influenced by radical Christian ideals had major problems with conservative congregations. A study of the Methodist congregation in Uralla, a town in the northern New South Wales tableland region, showed a succession of young ministers in the 1950s and 1960s arousing much hostility among the older middle class leadership of the church. The clergy committed crimes such as preaching about 'political' issues, challenging the legitimacy of the moral order and allowing their wives to opt out of the traditional role of unpaid congregational servant. One especially unpopular minister, who arrived in 1966, opposed the Vietnam War, which the lay people strongly supported, and urged the congregation actively to support the poorer people of the district, particularly those living on the fringe of the town in appalling conditions in an Aboriginal reserve. One layperson responded: 'Most people can manage nowadays, and if they can't their families can. We are flat out looking after our own'.[12]

Indeed, in 1969 a survey of 1138 Protestant clergy in Victoria by Norman Blaikie revealed a major gap between traditional expectations of ministry and new theological ideas. Many of these ministers' parishioners would have been horrified to learn that 48% of their cohort supported the Labor Party, rising to 59% of Methodists and Congregationalists and dropping to only 25% of Presbyterians who did not join the Uniting Church. Also 35% had pro-secular views, that is a belief in relating Christian thought to developments in the wider community. These secularists ranged from 46% of the Congregationalists to 21% of Baptists. Although the majority of the clergy still held conservative political and social views, there was a large minority who had been influenced by newer secularist and social justice ideology.[13]

However, Protestant radicalism had its limits. Not many Protestant clergy or laypeople spoke out against the Vietnam War in the early days of Australian military intervention. The executive committee of the Australian Council of Churches (ACC), the successor to the ACWCC, which covered the mainline and some smaller Protestant

* As a member of the 1964–65 Victorian Presbyterian Assemblies, I joined with other young clerical and lay members in a voting block that helped defeat the annual attempt by some older members to ban the consumption of alcoholic liquor on Presbyterian church property.

denominations plus Orthodox churches, expressed concern about illiberal conscientious objection provisions of the *National Service Act*. But it did not initially condemn Australia's involvement in the war. The pacifist Alf Dickie was one of the few early Presbyterian protesters. A Methodist who took an anti-war stand, the Rev. Douglas Trathen, headmaster of the elite Sydney Methodist boys' school, Newington College, was sacked by the school council when he recommended that young men should refuse to register for National Service. However, the New South Wales Methodist Church leadership, such as Alan Walker, supported Trathen and, after strong debate, the Methodist Conference in 1967 called for an immediate ceasefire in the war. At this time this was a novel resolution by any mainline Protestant denomination about Australian participation in warfare.

A surprising Anglican action came from the evangelical Anglican Bishop William Hardy of Ballarat, who had been an earlier contributor to the Anglican hysteria about the threat of Communism. In 1969 he spoke out in support of an imprisoned conscientious objector to 'a war which a very great number of Australians condemn as barbarous and inhuman'. He was joining a growing peace movement in Australia, which swelled into huge moratorium marches in 1970. But this movement was not influenced by Australian church leadership. It was responding to a peace movement already causing headaches to the political leaders of the United States, and was reacting to the ways in which the Tet offensive in South Vietnam in 1968 and the horrors of images of the war on television screens were sapping public confidence about the winnability and morality of the war. In 1970 conservative church opposition to this peace movement was indicated after Hardy told his diocesan synod that 'the murderous slaughter and mutilation of a whole people' by the United States must be halted immediately. For the first time in the history of the diocese the bishop's presidential address was greeted with stony silence.[14]

Within Roman Catholicism in the 1960s there was also a new radical force generated by the momentous Second Vatican Council of 1962. Edmund Campion explained: 'The Vatican II years were a springtime in Catholicism. To many it seemed that the church was at last shucking off outmoded accretions from the past'.[15] It was an era of more free thought and speech in the church, though bishops still tried to maintain clerical control. The new climate encouraged the opposition of some well-educated Catholics to the Vietnam War. It influenced a group of Catholic curates to challenge the septuagenarian Cardinal Gilroy to sanction new styles of team ministries.

The Australian Catholic episcopacy did not completely resist the changes. In 1969 the Australian Episcopal Conference (AEC) agreed to join with the mostly Protestant ACC in an inter-church conference in January 1970 which agreed to launch Action for World Development (AWD), a campaign to challenge Australian Christians about the injustices of hunger and poverty in the third world. This campaign in 1972 involved an estimated 150 000 people in the first ever joint Catholic-Protestant project in Australia. In Canberra, lay Catholics were in the forefront of AWD activity, expressing a new ecumenical zeal. But in the next year there was a dramatic collapse of Catholic involvement in follow-up AWD groups in Canberra and other dioceses in Australia because AWD had dared to criticise Australia's involvement in the Vietnam War. However, at the national level it retained Catholic financial support.

Despite this situation, Catholic radicalism was still alive. During the 1970s and early 1980s there was growing cooperation between the ACC's Commission for World Christian Action, which managed the overseas aid work of the member churches, and the organisers of the Catholic equivalent, Project Compassion. There was a common growth of social justice emphases in these bodies.

But the ACC was running into opposition, led by ultra-conservatives, for its involvement in the World Council of Churches' Program for Combatting Racism which was providing financial support for refugees in southern Africa. The League of Rights, an anti-semitic neo-fascist group, with significant Protestant church membership, was a major opponent of the ACC, accusing it of pro-Communist sympathy. Efforts, with probable South African Government financial support, were made to stop church people giving to the Christmas Bowl Appeal, the main money-raiser for ACC overseas programs. For example, stickers proclaiming that Christmas Bowl money bought bullets for Marxist terrorists were placed under windscreen wipers of cars parked outside churches on Sunday mornings. This propaganda did adversely affect Christmas Bowl funds, but the Appeal received the support of many, especially Uniting Church clergy, and was well supported by many parishes.

Likewise, another radical Catholic group, the Commission for Justice and Peace (CCJP) was coming under criticism for some social justice policies, especially support for Aborigines. It had been established by the AEC in 1968 in response to a Pontifical Commission for Justice and Peace, which was a result of the Second Vatican Council. In 1972, the CCJP was provided with its own staff and commission members, who were mostly well-educated laypeople appointed by state bishops and by a committee of the AEC. In 1981 the CCJP in company with the ACC, vigorously took up the cause of land rights for Aborigines, especially 'to raise the awareness of all church-goers on the Land Rights issue'.[16] However, CCJP money and assistance to empower Aborigines to challenge the claims of mining companies to Aboriginal land were the catalyst for conservative Catholic reaction. The complaints of mining companies scared many bishops, especially the conservative Cardinal James Freeman, who had been appointed as Gilroy's successor in 1971. The NCC was also circulating false propaganda about Marxist influence in the CCJP. The AEC closed the Commission down in 1987.

However, in the 1970s and through the 1980s, there was growing interdenominational cooperation in resistance to an ultra conservative Christian, Joh Bjelke-Petersen, Premier of Queensland from 1968 to 1988 and a practising Lutheran. Exploiting a gerrymander worse than the one introduced by Labor, his National Party government ruled with as little as 19% of the vote with, and at times without, the assistance of a supine Liberal Party. Street marches were abolished, libel suits throttled press criticism, and critics were labelled 'Communists' and 'ratbags'.

This government, ruled by a Premier who loved to preach Christian morality, was also poisoned by corruption to the level of the head of the police force and Cabinet members as revealed in the Fitzerald inquiry into police corruption. But the political opposition from the Labor Party, suffering from internal divisions, was ineffective. The Anglican Dean of the Brisbane Cathedral, Ian George, later said that for a time the church was the only viable opposition to the government.[17] Leaders of the Anglican and Uniting Churches, with some Catholic support, were active in the defence of free speech, advocacy for the rights of Queensland's Aborigines — still regimented by the 1897 *Protection Act* — and concern about environmental issues. However, it should be emphasised that this was cooperation by church leaders. Many Protestant and Catholic church people were happily voting for Bjelke-Petersen's National Party or directing their second preferences to it rather than to Labor. The ultimate success for opponents of the government was more the result of investigative television and press reporters and confessions by corrupt policemen, which exposed the government's protection of rampant corruption while posturing as the defender of law and order. This was the main reason for the Labor Party's sweeping election victory in 1989, though receiving only 54% of the preferred vote. Many church-going Christians in Queensland were still voting for the Liberal and National parties.

New deals for Aborigines

The support by some Queensland church leaders and by the CCJP and the ACC for Aboriginal rights in the 1980s was a symptom of a new Christian approach to Australia's indigenous population. Elkin's proposal for Aboriginal citizenship was implemented finally in a national referendum in 1967. Assisting the overwhelming affirmative vote was support by all political parties, and the NMCA program for improving attitudes towards Aborigines in churches helped. In the wider public arena NMCA's National Aborigines Day, which by the mid-1960s had become a public event with involvement of media personalities, public figures and Aborigines, was another awareness-raising process.

However, at the same time there were many Aborigines living in squalid conditions on the fringes of country towns, usually located in the worst possible position such as next to the rubbish tip. They were generally being ignored by local church people, such as the Methodists of Uralla. This prejudice was deeply entrenched. In the early 1980s in a western New South Wales town called 'Brindletown' in Gillian Cowlishaw's study, Anglicans, who constituted 30% of the community and who were were almost all white, paid no attention to the Aborigines who varied from a fifth to a third of the town's population and lived in much worse conditions than the whites. Only the Catholic Church, with an unusually high 40% of the population, had a large number of Aboriginal parishioners.[18] The town's Europeans maintained an informal colour bar against social contact with Aborigines, and the town council's main attention to them was to suppress disorderly behaviour.

The radical promise of Alfred Clint's cooperative movement was also blighted by conservative Anglican opposition in the 1960s. In 1961 S. J. Matthews, the new Anglican Bishop of Carpentaria, considered Clint a destabilising influence among Aborigines. The National Party Queensland Government accused him of being a Communist and prohibited his entry into government-controlled Aboriginal reserves and missions. However, he continued to promote cooperatives in the cause of Aboriginal self-reliance but with little success because of the lack of government and church support. Matthews and senior mission staff perceived the cooperatives as giving Aborigines false ideas of independence from mission and government supervision.

Indeed, in Christian mission work in the early 1960s paternalism was still the general order of the day. It took action by Aborigines themselves to make major changes. Soon after the anthropologically-trained Methodist minister, Edgar Wells, arrived in 1961 at the Milingimbi mission in Arnhem Land in the Northern Territory, some of the local Yirrkala people approached him with anxiety about mining exploration which was taking place under the terms of the agreement signed by the mission in 1958. However, the secretary of the Methodist Board of Mission, Cecil Gribble, insisted on honouring the agreement and proposed moving the mission station away from the mining area. Wells protested in vain about the attachment of the Yirrkala people to their land and their concern about destruction of sacred sites.

In 1963 the Yirrkala people sent a bark painting, with a petition in the Aboriginal language in its centre, to the Commonwealth Parliament at the suggestion of an Anglican Labor member, Kim Beazley, who visited the area. Evidence taken from the Yirrkala people in their own language and from Wells resulted in a Parliamentary Committee recommending that they should be consulted before any mining began. But the LCP Commonwealth Government did not act on this report. It had signed a $50 million lease with Gove Bauxite Company and was determined that Aborigines should not stand in the way of economic development, using the justification that mining operations would benefit their assimilation into European society. The mission's response was to transfer Wells from the mission station. It also soon became known that the Methodist Church held investments in a Queensland mining company. Gribble commented to Wells: 'We must learn to live with the idea of mining in the reserve. After all, it is our capitalist way of doing things'.[19]

The Yirrkala bark petition, which achieved much publicity, did not prevent mining on their land. However, it sparked a change of church thinking about Aboriginal land rights. In 1965 the ACC published *Land Rights for Aboriginal People* setting out a new approach which rejected assimilation and advocated allowing Aborigines to develop in their own way on their own land. In 1969 the Methodist Board of Mission indicated its about-turn by supporting Aboriginal land ownership, including mineral rights, which was endorsed by the Methodist Church and soon by the Presbyterian, Congregational and Anglican churches. Action followed words, with Uniting Church ministers being arrested in 1980 for standing alongside the Yungngara people protesting at oil drilling on their land at Noonkambah in northwest Western Australia. That protest, which was supported by the heads of the Western Australian Catholic, Anglican, and Uniting Churches, indicated their acceptance of Aboriginal spirituality. One of the arrested ministers explained: 'To this place the Aboriginal would belong and to this place his spirit would return on his death on its way to the Dreamtime. To destroy such a site would be to destroy his link with eternity'.[20]

It was still necessary to abandon the paternalistic notion that Europeans knew best for Aborigines. At the ACC general meeting in Brisbane in 1982 an important motion was proposed to grant autonomous decision-making to an Aboriginal Development Commission. Some delegates had been appointed by their churches to vote against that motion. But on the day for discussion, Aboriginal members of the Commission spoke with such reasonableness and eloquence, that the motion was easily passed. However, it had to wait until 1989 before the ACC set up an Aboriginal and Islander Commission with only Aboriginal and Islander members and with complete autonomy in the expenditure of money. By then churches had taken the first steps to hand back land to Aborigines, starting with the General Assembly of the Uniting Church in 1979, and followed by the Catholic and Anglican Churches. Also in 1975 the Catholic Church was the last of the mainline churches to ordain an Aboriginal priest, Patrick Dodson. In 1985 the Rev. Djiniyini Gondarra was installed in Darwin as the first Uniting Church moderator of its Northern Synod. That year Arthur Malcolm was consecrated in Townsville, Queensland, as the first Aboriginal Anglican bishop. The changed attitudes of the mainline churches towards Aborigines was demonstrated by their condemnation in 1993 of racist hysteria generated by mining companies and some non-Labor politicians in reaction to the High Court's Mabo decision, which acknowledged that Torres Strait Islanders and Aborigines had a legitimate claim to land with which they have had constant association.

Christianity has benefited from the handing back of land and religious authority to Aboriginal people and the church's acceptance of their spirituality and land rights. The establishment of the Aboriginal Evangelical Fellowship (AEF) by Aboriginal Christians in 1971 signified the emergence of Aboriginal Christianity. Despite some mission opposition and a financial struggle, the AEF concentrated on training Aboriginal leaders and in 1982 started organising regional conventions. At the second one held that year at the former Presbyterian mission station of Ernabella in northern South Australia, there were no non-Aboriginal speakers. There has been a great expansion of Christianity among Aborigines. A spiritual revival in 1978 on Elcho Island in the Northern Territory was another major event in the process. Aboriginal Christianity has a strong evangelical flavour, stemming from the style of most Christian missions. The music used by the AEF, such as its song book, *Gospel Favourites Along the Murray*, includes hymns and choruses that were beloved by evangelical missionaries. But much of this Christianity also relates to Aboriginal beliefs in the supernatural and respects the strong spiritual bonds between Aborigines and land.

The spread of Aboriginal Christianity in the post-mission age has been a phenomenon matched in Africa and in Asia, especially Korea. But it was notable for communities who have been oppressed by Christian Europeans. The Katetye people of Central Australia have suffered two savage massacres, one in 1874 following an attack on the Barrow Creek Telegraph Station—which they say was caused by interference with Aboriginal women—and the Consiton massacre of 1928. Yet in the 1990s, most say they are Christians. One of them, Peter Horsetailer, simply explained: 'We believe in one God'.[21] They had previously only sporadic contact with Lutheran missionaries from the Hermannsburg mission, and for a couple of years in the early 1970s a Lutheran Islander pastor lived among them. They have maintained their own faith since. But most Katetye people, including young ones, have parallel beliefs in Aboriginal spirituality. Evidence of this is present day fears that a mining venture will destroy sacred sites and threaten their world view.

Furthermore, there has been some unifying of Christianity and Aboriginal spirituality. Christian corroborees, called Jesus purlapa, were first performed in 1978 by the Warlpiri people of Yuendumu in the Northern Territory and have widely spread through Aboriginal communities across northern and central Australia. They use 'traditional body paint, dance motions and melodies', but the subject matter is Christian, such as the Easter story.[22] This syncretism has not been easily accepted by conservative Church leaders. 'Pat' Dodson broke with the Catholic Church in 1981 when Jan O'Loghlin, the Bishop of Darwin, said he could tolerate, but not approve 'pagan' intrusions into Christianity. Dodson was trying to integrate traditional Aboriginal culture 'with Christian celebratory practices'.[23] How many Aborigines identify themselves as Christian is unknown. Many living in urban regions are now only nominal Christians, like the majority of white Australians. Only 4330 people in the Australian census of 1991 said they were adherents of Aboriginal tribal religions.

Certainly, some present day mission-trained Aborigines have rejected Christianity. One is song writer Kevin Carmody. He was born in Cairns and grew up in southern Queensland, where he was taught an Aboriginal spirituality based on 'the enormity of the universe', principally by older Aboriginal women in a community that had been divorced from sacred land sites by the cattle industry. At the age of ten he was taken with his brother to an orphanage where the Catholic nuns 'strapped you for everything', imposing a Christian religion based on fear. But he and his brother would slip out at night to feel the wind on their faces and gaze at the moon and stars and realign themselves with their universe-based Aboriginal spirituality. His was an example of the strength of that spirituality which has for the past two centuries resisted Christianity. In 1988 'Kev' Carmody first came to Australian public attention as a writer of songs with cutting criticism of white society. He utilises his Catholic upbringing by employing strong Christian symbolism. He sings about the Christian Church's 'magnificent message' that white Australians do not want to hear—of 'comrade' Jesus Christ, the champion of the poor and the oppressed.

Women and Christian churches

In a recent article, Anne O'Brien argues how the churches were influential in the perpetuation of masculine values in Australia.[24] In efforts to get men back into church where there were majorities of women, there was a stress on boys' and men's organisations such as the Methodist Order of Knights, the Church of England Boys Society, and the Catholic Young Men's Societies. These organisations perpetuated male clannishness. Churches preached the value of hearth and home with women serving the needs of their men folk, and Catholic women were subject to frequent child bearing. Protestant clergy's wives were expected to perform dual roles of dutiful housewife and parish worker, to the point of rebellion in the 1950s and 1960s, as indicated by the Methodist ministers' wives in Uralla who faced trenchant opposition from laypeople — male and female.

The Christian churches certainly contributed to the masculine dominance of Australian society. However, they were not the only such force. The predominance of men in Australia's early population, the bush ethos — even though more image than actuality — and the general conservativeness of Australian society were factors. It was not only the fault of churches that in 1971 fewer than 10% of the female workforce were employers or self-employed, only 1% of Australian university professors were women, no woman headed a government public service department, and there were very few women in State and Federal Parliaments. It was the early 1970s when Australian women, such as Germaine Greer and Anne Summers, started to attack the manifest sexual inequality in Australian life. So it was not surprising that in 1976 the last Methodist Church General Conference had only twelve women in its 192 members, and the Presbyterian General Assembly eight women and 538 men. Indeed, within the Australian churches women had started agitating for change as early as 1968 with the foundation of a Christian feminist group; and the ACC had responded in 1973 with the establishment of a Commission on the Status of Women.

However, effecting change in the dominant male culture was no easy task. One of the foremost female activists in the founding of the Uniting Church, Dorothy McMahon, said: 'it was a very hard struggle even to get a women's issue on the agenda'.[25] A requirement was established that all councils and committees of the new church should include at least one third of women. But at the Uniting Church's General Assembly in 1985 this prescription was dropped, despite a survey of parishes and presbyteries revealing that women rarely constituted more than 30% of their councils and committees. At that stage only 4% of Uniting Church ministers were women. Indeed, women ministers still faced difficulties in acceptance by Uniting Church parishes.*

* At the beginning of the 1990s I knew a female minister who left her parish because of her parishioners' inability to accept her, and another parish, which deliberately replaced a single woman minister with a married man.

This conservativeness was demonstrated by the struggle in the Anglican church for the ordination of women priests well after its achievement in Anglican churches in New Zealand and Canada. After failing repeatedly to achieve the necessary two-thirds majority in the General Synod of Australia, Bishop Owen Dowling of the Canberra Goulburn diocese tried to buck the church's legal system by ordaining eleven women in December 1991. He was stopped by a strident group opposing women priests which obtained a restraining court order. The impasse was not broken until a special general synod meeting in 1992 narrowly resolved to allow dioceses to make their own decision. This produced a rash of ordinations of Anglican women priests across Australia, but certainly not in the evangelical Sydney Diocese.

Non-Christian religions

The 1991 Australian census revealed the greatly increased religious diversity which had arisen from the ever changing ethnic composition of post-war migration. People claiming non-Christian religions now comprised 2.6% of the population, compared with 0.5% in 1947 and 1.4% in 1981. In 1991 the biggest non-Christian groups were the 147505 Muslims (0.9%) and 139795 Buddhists (0.8%), relegating Judaism (0.4%) to third place.[26]

The major source of new Muslim immigrants has been Turkey. Turkish religious life in Australia has been affected by the instability of a society infected by a 'guest worker' mentality and problems of adjusting to an overwhelming non-Islamic community. But Turkish immigrants founded religious associations such as the Turkish Islamic Society in Melbourne, established in 1970. By the late 1980s they had more religious bodies like the Turkish Islamic Cultural Centre in Sydney, which provide cultural, religious and language classes on evenings and weekends. They are also involved in the delivery of welfare services, but rely on Turkish community financial support because of minimal government funding. Because Turkish Muslims come from an Islamic country with a secular state, there is a general absence of Islamic fundamentalism in Australia. Yet they and other Islamic immigrants from former Yugoslavia, Albania, the Lebanon, other Middle Eastern countries, the Indian sub-continent, Malaysia and Indonesia have faced discrimination from local councils when applying for land for mosques. Some suffered violent persecution during the Gulf War of 1991 in an Australian xenophobic reaction against 'Arabs' even though most Arab countries were western allies and most Australian Muslims are not Arabs.

The principal cause of the big increase of the Buddhist population has been the influx of refugees and migrants from Vietnam. In 1986 people born in Vietnam comprised 0.5% of the Australian population and as many as 4.2% of people in the Fairfield-Liverpool region of suburban Sydney. Along with immigrants from Cambodia and children born in Australia, Buddhists comprised 4.8% of the population in that Sydney region.[27] Trickles of migration from other southeastern Asian nations have contributed to the Buddhist population, as has a new influx of Chinese. But many Chinese Buddhists do not privately practice the faith. Some post-Christian Australians, in search of exotic spirituality in the increasingly materialistic Australian society, have also been attracted to Buddhism.

Some locally-born Australians are followers of another religion brought to Australia by Asian immigrants, especially refugees from religious persecution in Iran. They are the 7484 adherents of the Baha'a Faith. This religion is a by-product of Iranian Islam, which is based on a transcendent God, and has spread since the mid-nineteenth century around the world. Another more significant Asian religion in Australia followed in 1991 by 43 580 people is the Hindu religion (0.3%). There were also 7795 Sikhs. These two religious groups were formed as part of an Indian migration.

After the Second World War pre-war prejudice had continued about Jewish immigration with an outburst of anti-semitism in the press and parliament. Immigration Minister Calwell responded by terminating a program to admit 2000 refugees who had survived German prison camps, after the first few arrived in Australia. There was continued discrimination against Jewish refugees in the big post-war migration program, though some Australian Jews acted to stop German migration because of the danger of importing ex-Nazis. German and Austrian Jews, especially 2542 sent from England and Australia on the *Dunera*, had been interned during the war. On their post-war release many achieved later high status in Australia as doctors, academics, musicians and businessmen.

There was an influx of Eastern European Jews after the war which weakened the Anglo-Jewish dominance and increased the Jewish proportion of Australia's population to 0.56% in 1961. Notable areas of Jewish strength were St Kilda and Caulfield in Melbourne and

Waverley and Randwick in Sydney. In 1986, 5.2% of the population of Sydney's Eastern suburbs was Jewish, and there the Jewish vote has electoral relevance. Since the immediate post-war era there has been a decline of anti-semitism, but the League of Rights and neo-Nazis have kept it alive. There was also anti-semitism in the 'socialist left' of the Labor party. There have been occasional violent attacks on synagogues. However, Australian foreign policy has been pro-Israel, with a well organised and noisy Jewish lobby, as any politicians who dare to question that stance know very well. Australia has also had a Jewish Governor General from 1977 to 1982 — Zelman Cowen was the Australian born son of a Russian Jewish refugee in England. However, in the 1990s like Christianity, the Jewish faith is suffering from the secularisation of Australian society. This has encouraged an ultra-orthodox reaction among a minority, but has weakened the allegiance of the many more 'liberal' Jews. Increasing marriage with non-Jews and consequent 'acculturalisation' of these families has led to a decline in the Jewish proportion of the Australian population in the three decades after 1961.

Christianity in the 1990s

The 1991 Australian census also indicated major changes in the Christian community in Australia. One phenomenon is the growth rate of census-Catholics, initially fuelled by immigration of Catholics from Europe and boosted by new migrants from the Philippines and Latin America. From 26% of Australia's population in 1981, Catholics have increased to 27.3%. At the same time Anglicans, not benefiting from recent migration and losing people to the 'no-religion' category, have declined from 26.1% to 23.9%. For the first time in Australian history, Catholicism had become the largest religious denomination. An earlier major Christian change was the ever growing proportion of people of the many branches of the Orthodox Christian faith generated by migrations from Eastern Europe and the Middle East. Prior to the post-Second World War wave of migration to Australia, these members of one of the great branches of Christianity — the Orthodox churches of Eastern Europe and the Middle East — were only small in number in Australia: 0.3% of the population in 1947. Their proportion then grew from 1.5% in 1961 to 3% in 1981. However, the slackening of that migration and early signs of secularisation of the Orthodox community caused its proportion to dip to 2.8% in 1991.

Nevertheless, Orthodox Christianity was the fifth largest religious group in Australia, behind Presbyterian and reformed Christians.

A striking feature of the 1991 census, however, was a turnaround in the decline of Christian faith in Australia. Major religious denominations had grown at a greater rate since 1986 than the 7.9% population increase, ranging from Orthodox (11.1%) to Baptists (42.3%). Most denominations had grown at a faster rate than the 9.1% increase of the 13% of Australians who stated they had no religion. The Christian churches missing out were Anglicans, who marked time, plus the Salvation Army (-7.4%) and Churches of Christ (-11.8%), two latter-day religious arrivals in Australia which enjoyed no ethnic identity.[28]

Part of the reason for the faster growth rate in publicly-acknowledged religious identity may have been the tick in a box method of religious choice. However, this does not measure the disparity between increases in 'no religion' and most of the Christian denominations. There is also a gap between census growth rates, membership figures and attendance at worship. The Uniting Church, which grew by 17.4%, has experienced a steady decline in membership numbers. However, the 1991 National Church Life Survey, which covered 305 000 Australian Protestants, demonstrated an increase in weekly attendances at Uniting Churches from 1986 by 8.1%, just above the population growth rate. There was greater growth in weekly attendance in the more evangelical, Pentecostal and fundamentalist smaller Protestant groups by 12% to 15%. By contrast, only 22% of Catholics in 1991 attended church weekly compared with 54% in 1961 and 36% of Baptists in 1991.[29]

The non-mainline Protestant growth in the 1980s and early 1990s was part of a religious revival in Australia. Its strength was particularly in Pentecostal and evangelical congregations, where religious enthusiasm and fundamentalist theology have provided a refuge for victims of economic recession and the vicissitudes of rapid social change. In the Uniting Church, the growth rate has been more in the minority of Pentecostal parishes rather than in the more liberal ones, which are still participating in the general decline. The National Life survey showed that of the people surveyed, 3% had converted to Christianity in the past five years and 5% were lapsed Christians who had returned to church attendance since 1986. Women still outnumbered male Protestants, but not as much as is imagined: a ratio of ten to eight. Only the Orthodox Christians, Buddhists and Muslims had more men, which related to their theological traditions. Catholics and

Protestants in 1991 were older than average, suggesting that when the revival peters out, Christianity may suffer more decline in Australia.

Also the general conservativeness of Protestant Australian Christians in 1991 was measured by the fact that only 3% of them were involved in social action/social justice groups in the wider community. Many more (22%) were involved in traditional social care activities. But the majority took no part in wider community action. There was a big gap between the radicalism of Uniting Church, Anglican and Catholic spokespeople—who in 1992 helped convince the leader of the Liberal Party, John Hewson, to remove the projected tax on food from his consumption tax package—and the people in church pews. Opinion polling about the 1990 federal election, which was won by Labor, showed 60% of weekly church-attenders voting for the LNP.[30]

Summary

From the 1960s to the 1990s Australia was transformed into a post-Christian society. Protestant churches lost their previous political power, and in many cases the will which had imposed the quiet Sunday on cities such as Melbourne and Adelaide into the 1960s, which also until that decade banned pictures of naked bodies on film screens, and which kept hotels closed after 6.00 p.m. and on Sundays. The Catholic Church completed its divorce with the Labor Party because of state aid to schools. A majority of Australians had ceased attending churches. Many weddings were being conducted outside church buildings by secular marriage celebrants. Even funerals were deserting churches for crematorium chapels, although usually, for this older Australian generation, clergy officiated. The small religious revival of the 1980s has not changed the process of secularisation of Australian society. Religion was no longer part of the political rhetoric as in the Menzies era. Politicians, particularly of the 'new right', were appealing to the cult of selfishness and the collapse of the religious moral order was observable in rising crime rates and declining standards of business and public probity.

Chapter Seven

Conclusion

One of the most important areas of the influence of religion in Australia has been political developments. Australian politics have been constantly affected into the 1960s by the issue of state aid for Catholic schools — used by Protestants to defeat Catholic-led governments and a major factor in the 1965 New South Wales State election. Catholic influence was an important feature of Labor Party history, not only the Movement and the split in the 1950s, but also as an earlier bulwark against socialism. The ability of the Catholic community, with mostly less than a quarter of the Australian population, to provide a majority of Ministers of many Labor governments was a major achievement. Even after the Labor split in the 1950s, the Catholic-influenced DLP was able to assist in perpetuating conservative Commonwealth governments until 1972.

The important influence of Protestantism in non-Labor parties is often overlooked. From the earliest days of Australian political history, anti-Catholicism was an important element in non-Labor party propaganda. As late as the New South Wales election of 1922, it was a major factor in the electoral defeat of Labor. The decline of sectarianism was influenced by waning Protestant religious enthusiasm, but as late as the 1950s the Menzies Government used Protestant ideology in its political philosophy.

The major thrust of Protestant involvement in politics has been to support the conservative status quo. Only a small minority of Protestants were involved in early Labor politics and even fewer were socialists. The Protestant and Catholic churches showed their conservative face with largely palliative attempts to cope with the distress of the depressions of the 1890s and 1930s, rather than challenging the capitalist order. In Australia's wars, Protestant churches have been strong supporters of the imperial and national causes, with Catholics generally providing similar support, even in the First World War. Only in the Vietnam War was there significant religious dissent, but it mostly followed the rise of a public peace movement. Radicals within Australian churches always had minority status. Even with the development of social justice thought after the Second World War, the majority of clergy remained conservative, and regular Church-attenders voted heavily for non-Labor political parties.

Conservative paternalism was also the predominant missionary attitude towards Aborigines. Not until the 1960s was there a major change, and this was influenced by new Aboriginal assertiveness. In the post-mission Aboriginal community there has been new Christian growth with syncretic experiments between Christianity and resilient Aboriginal spirituality. This spirituality gave Aborigines the ability to resist Christianity, and survive mission attempts to eradicate it. This was also helped by the fact that missions never controlled a majority of Australia's Aboriginal population.

The other major influence of religion in Australian history was its contribution to moral order, initially to counter the licentiousness of the convict community and then as a crusade to create a holy nation. The Christian moral order was not achieved because of divisions within Protestant ranks and opposition by secularists and at times by Catholics. However, there were some successes — the quiet Sundays, sexual prudishness, reductions in the hours and outlets for selling alcohol and restriction of public gambling facilities. Christianity, Catholic as well as Protestant, was also responsible for a general rise in the emphasis on 'respectability' in the middle classes and for socially ambitious workers. It also influenced a dramatic fall in crime rates in Australia by the 1890s. At that time only about a quarter of the population was separated from the church. A majority of adults in Victoria and South Australia, and nearly a majority in New South Wales, attended churches regularly.

The twentieth century saw a general erosion of this moral order accompanied by a decline in church attendance. But the fall in church allegiance was not as great as has been imagined. In the 1950s nearly half the Australian population, and a majority of middle class people, had regular attachment to churches. Only the degree of regularity of attendance had substantially changed. The irregularity was a sign of waning religious commitment. This had hampered evangelical efforts to impose alcoholic prohibition on Australian States and to prevent the erosion of sabbatarianism. But Australia in the 1950s was still a morally conservative society. The Catholic Church, with its puritanical Irish face, played its part in maintaining this moral order even though it was more relaxed about drinking, gambling and the use of Sundays for purposes other than worship.

The 1960s saw the beginning of the collapse of Christian morality in an increasingly secular Australian society, though the emergence of secular Christianity also sapped Christian moral energy. While Australia was predominantly irreligious in the first decades of European settlement, religion was then an integral part of the colonial state. Not until the 1960s did Australia start to become a post-Christian society, where religion no longer has the same degree of power it once enjoyed to influence political events.

Modern Australia also has more religious diversity with the growth of non-Christian religions, especially Islam and Buddhism. This is in addition to Judaism, which was the only significant former non-Christian religion, apart from Aboriginal spirituality. However, non-Christian religious sects are still only a small minority of the Australian population and are likely to face future problems of secularism and absorption into the dominant Christian religious culture.

Notes

Preface

1 A.C. Bouquet, *Comparative Religion: A Short Outline*, Penguin, Harmondsworth, 1969, p. 16.

2 Michael Hogan, *The Sectarian Strand: Religion in Australian History*, Penguin, Sydney, 1987. Ian Breward, *A History of the Australian Churches*, Allen & Unwin, Sydney 1993.

1. Christianity and Early European Settlement

1 Jean Woolmington (ed.), *Religion in Early Australia: The Problem of Church and State*, Cassell, Sydney, 1976, p. 1.

2 Neil K. Macintosh, *Richard Johnson: Chaplain to the Colony of New South Wales. His Life and Times 1755–1827*, Pilgrim International, Sydney, 1978, p. 54.

3 Allan M. Grocott, *Convicts, Clergymen and Churches: Attitudes of Convicts and Ex-Convicts towards the Churches and Clergy in New South Wales from 1788 to 1851*, Sydney University Press, Sydney, 1980, p. 66.

4 Robert Dixon, *The Course of Empire: Neo-Classical Culture in New South Wales 1788–1860*, Oxford University Press, Melbourne, 1986, pp. 22, 24.

5 John Harris, *One Blood. 200 Years of Aboriginal Encounter with Christianity: A Story of Hope*, Albatross Books, Sutherland, 1990, p. 22.

6 Harris, *One Blood*, p. 54.

7 Edmund Campion, *Australian Catholics*, Penguin, Ringwood, 1987, p. 12.

8 Wray Vamplew (ed.), *Australians: Historical Statistics*, Fairfax, Syme & Weldon, Sydney, 1987, p. 421.

9 Woolmington, *Religion in Early Australia*, p. 150.

10 Russel Ward and John Robertson (eds), *Such was Life: Select Documents in Australian Social History*, Alternative Publishing Company, Chippendale, 1978, vol. 1, p. 325.

11 Hogan, *The Sectarian Strand*, p. 45; *Australian Dictionary of Biography* (*ADB*), vol.2, Melbourne University Press, Melbourne, 1967, p. 588.

12 Alan Atkinson and Marian Aveling (eds), *Australians 1838*, Fairfax, Syme & Weldon, Sydney, 1987, p. 425.
13 Atkinson and Aveling, *Australians 1838*, p. 429.
14 G.P. Shaw, *Patriarch and Patriot: William Grant Broughton 1788–1853*, Melbourne University Press, Melbourne, 1978, p. 125.
15 John Barrett, *That Better Country: The Religious Aspect of Life in Eastern Australia, 1835–1850*, Melbourne University Press, Melbourne, 1966, p. 169.

2 Challenges to Protestant Ascendancy

1 Barrett, *That Better Country*, p. 196.
2 D.W.A. Baker, *Days of Wrath: A Life of John Dunmore Lang*, Melbourne University Press, Melbourne, 1985, p. 354.
3 A.G. Austin, *Australian Education 1788–1900: Church, State and Public Education in Colonial Australia*, Pitman, Melbourne, 1961, p.156.
4 Arnold D. Hunt, *This Side of Heaven: A History of Methodism in South Australia*, Lutheran Publishing House, Adelaide, 1985, p. 179.
5 *ADB*, vol. 4, p. 396.
6 G.R. Quaife, 'Religion and Colonial Politics: State Aid and Sectarianism in Victoria, 1856', *Journal of Religious History*, vol. 10, 1978, p. 198.
7 Robert Travers, *The Phantom Fenians of New South Wales*, Kangaroo Press, Sydney, 1986, p. 161.
8 F.B. Smith, 'Spiritualism in Victoria in the Nineteenth Century', *Journal of Religious History*, 3, 1965, p. 247.
9 Walter Phillips, *Defending 'A Christian Century': Churchmen and Society in New South Wales in the 1880s and After*, University of Queensland Press, St Lucia, 1981, p.171; Vamplew, pp. 26, 421–2.
10 Geoffrey Serle, *The Rush to be Rich: A History of the Colony of Victoria*, Melbourne University Press, Melbourne, 1971, p. 152; Walter Phillips, 'Religious Profession and Practice in N.S.W., 1850–1901: The Statistical Evidence', *Historical Studies*, vol. 15, No. 59, 1972, pp. 385–90; Eric Richards (ed.), *The Flinders History of South Australia: Social History*, Wakefield Press, Adelaide, 1986, p. 218.
11 Patricia Grimshaw, 'Family and Community in Nineteenth-Century Castlemaine' in Patrica Grimshaw, Chris McConville & Ellen McEwen (eds), *Families in Colonial Australia*, Allen & Unwin, Sydney, 1985, pp. 83–104.
12 Serle, *The Rush to be Rich*, p. 138.
13 A.J.C. Mayne, *Fever, Squalor and Vice: Sanitation and Social Policy in Victorian Sydney*, University of Queensland Press, St Lucia, 1982, p. 109.
14 Brian Kennedy, *Silver, Sin and Sixpenny Ale: A Social History of Broken Hill 1883–1921*, Melbourne University Press, Melbourne, 1978, pp. 25–6, 45–8.
15 Arthur M. Schlesinger, Sr., 'A Critical Period in American Religion, 1875–1900' in John M. Mulder and John F. Wilson (eds), *Religion in American History: Interpretive Essays*, Prentice Hall, Englewood Cliffs, 1978, p. 307.
16 Michael Sturma, *Vice in a Vicious Society: Crime and Convicts in Mid-Nineteenth Century New South Wales*, University of Queensland Press, St Lucia, 1983, p.188; Satyanshu K. Mukherjee, John R. Walker and Evelyn N. Jacobsen,

Crime and Punishment in the Colonies: A Statistical Profile, History Project Inc., Kensington, 1988, p. 120.

17 Roslyn Otzen, 'The Doorstep Evangelist: William Hall in Darkest Prahran' in Graeme Davison, David Dunston, and Chris McConville (eds), *The Outcasts of Melbourne: Essays in Social History*, Allen & Unwin, Sydney, 1985, p. 121.

18 Harris, *One Blood*, pp. 115–16.

19 M.F. Christie, *Aborigines in Colonial Victoria 1835–86*, Sydney University Press, Sydney, 1979, p. 40.

20 Dom Rosendo Salvado, *The Salvado Memoirs*, ed. E.J. Stormon, University of Western Australia Press, Nedlands, 1977, p. 103.

21 Muriel Berman, 'Bishop Salvado: A Reappraisal' in Bob Reece and Tom Stannage (eds), *European–Aboriginal Relations, in Western Australian History*, University of Western Australia Press, Nedlands, 1984. p. 39.

22 Noel Loos, 'The Australian Board of Missions, the Anglican Church and the Aborigines 1850–1900', *Journal of Religious History*, vol. 17, 1992, pp. 205–6.

23 J.B. Gribble, *Dark Deeds in a Sunny Land or Blacks and Whites in North-West Australia*, revised ed., University of Western Australia Press, Nedlands, 1987, p. 2.

3 Social Justice and Moral Order

1 John Rickard, *Class and Politics: New South Wales, Victoria and the Early Commonwealth*, Australian National University Press, Canberra, 1976, p. 65.

2 Ronald Lawson, *Brisbane in the 1890s: A Study of an Australian Urban Society*, University of Queensland Press, St Lucia, 1973, p. 297.

3 Hunt, *This Side of Heaven*, p. 205.

4 Phillips, *Defending 'A Christian Century'*, p. 163.

5 Don Wright and Eric Clancy, *The Methodists: A History of Methodism in New South Wales*, Allen & Unwin, Sydney, 1993, p. 106

6 Anne O'Brien, *Poverty's Prison: The Poor in New South Wales 1880–1918*, Melbourne University Press, Melbourne, 1988, p. 192.

7 P. J. O'Farrell, 'The History of the New South Wales Labour Movement, 1880–1914: A Religious Interpretation', *Journal of Religious History*, vol. 2, 1962, p. 142.

8 J. D. Bollen, *Protestantism and Social Reform in New South Wales 1890–1910*, Melbourne University Press, Melbourne, 1972, p. 77.

9 Patrick O'Farrell, *The Catholic Church and Community in Australia: A History*, Thomas Nelson, Sydney, 1977, p. 288.

10 Neil J. Byrne, *Robert Dunne: Archbishop of Brisbane,* University of Queensland Press, St Lucia, 1991, p. 196.

11 John Wanna, 'A Paradigm of Consent: Explanations of Working Class Moderation in South Australia', *Labour History*, No. 53, 1987, pp. 63–4.

12 Julie-Ann Ellis, '"Cross-Firing Over the Gulf." The Rift Between Methodism and the Labour Movement in South Australia in the 1890s', *Labour History*, No. 64, 1993, p. 94.

13 Rosslyn Reed, 'Calvinism, the Weber Thesis, and Entrepreneurial Behaviour: The Case of David Syme', *Journal of Religious History*, vol. 16, 1991, pp. 292–303.
14 Anthea Hyslop, 'Christian Temperance and Social Reform: The Women's Christian Temperance Movement of Victoria, 1887–1912' in Sabine Willis (ed.), *Women and Fetes: Essays on the History of Women and the Church in Australia*, Dove Communications, Melbourne, 1977, p. 47.
15 Diane Kirkby, *Alice Henry: The Power of Pen and Voice. The Life of an Australian-American Labor Reformer*, Cambridge University Press, Cambridge, 1991, pp. 48–9.
16 Richard Ely, *Unto God and Caesar: Religious Issues in the Emerging Commonwealth, 1891–1906*, Melbourne University Press, Melbourne, 1976, pp 10–11.
17 Ely, *Unto God and Caesar*, p. 34.
18 Vamplew, *Historical Statistics*, pp. 26, 421–6.
19 Walter Phillips, 'Religious Profession and Practice in N.S.W', pp. 385–90.
20 Richard Broome, *Treasure in Earthen Vessels: Protestant Christianity in New South Wales Society 1900–1914*, University of Queensland Press, St Lucia, 1980, p. 1.
21 Stuart Piggin, *Faith of Steel: A History of the Christian Churches in Illawarra, Australia*, University of Wollongong Press, Wollongong, 1984, p. 136.
22 Broome, *Treasure in Earthen Vessels*, pp. 68-70; Vamplew, pp. 26, 421, 428.
23 Bollen, *Protestantism and Social Reform*, p. 89.
24 Hunt, *This Side of Heaven*, p. 272.
25 Broome, *Treasure in Earthen Vessels*, p. 155.
26 Broome, *Treasure in Earthen Vessels*, pp. 98–9, 100.
27 Rickard, *Class and Politics*, p. 200.
28 Wright and Clancy, *The Methodists*, p. 102. L.M. Field, *The Forgotten War: Australian Involvement in the South African Conflict of 1899–1902*, Melbourne University Press, Melbourne, 1979, p. 45.
29 Field, *The Forgotten War*, p. 69.
30 Patrick Ford, *Cardinal Moran and the A.L.P.*, Melbourne University Press, Melbourne, 1966, p. 253.
31 A. E. Cahill, 'Catholics and Socialism: The 1905 Controversy in Australia', *Journal of Religious History*, vol. 1, 1960, pp. 88–99.
32 Celia Hamilton, 'Irish Catholics of New South Wales and the Labor Party, 1890–1910', *Historical Studies; Australia and New Zealand*, 8, 1958, p. 265.
33 A.E. Dingle, 'The Truly Magnificent Thirst: An Historical Survey of Australian Drinking Habits', *Historical Studies*, 19, 1980, p. 246.
34 Robert C. Bannister, *Social Darwinism: Science and Myth in Anglo-American Social Thought*, Temple University Press, Philadelphia, 1979, p. 181.
35 Earnest Gribble, *Forty Years with the Aborigines*, Angus & Robertson, Sydney, 1930, p. 122.
36 A. K. Chase, 'Lazarus at Australia's Gateway: The Christian Mission Enterprise in Eastern Cape York Peninsula' in Tony Swain and Deborah Bird Rose (eds), *Aboriginal Australians and Christian Missions: Ethnographic and Historical Studies*, Australian Association for the Study of Religion, Bedford Park, 1988, p. 125.
37 *ADB*, vol. 12, p. 250. William Thorpe, 'Archibald Meston and Aboriginal Legislation in Colonial Queensland', *Historical Studies*, vol. 21, 1984, p. 63.

38 Henry Reynolds, *Aborigines and Settlers*, Cassell, Melbourne, 1972, p. 67.
39 Harris, *One Blood*, p. 543.

4. Christian Conservatism

1 Michael McKernan, *Australian Churches at War: Attitudes and Activities of the Major Churches, 1914–1918*, Southwood Press, Sydney, 1980, p. 29.
2 John A. Moses, 'Canon David John Garland and the ANZAC Tradition', *St Mark's Review*, No. 54, 1993, p. 21, note 35.
3 McKernan, *Australian Churches at War*, p. 30.
4 Information from the First AIF data base, Department of History, University College, Australian Defence Force Academy, Canberra.
5 Ian Harmstorf and Michael Cigler, *The Germans in Australia*, AE Press, Melbourne, 1985, p. 127.
6 First AIF data base.
7 D. J. Murphy, *T. J. Ryan: A Political Biography*, University of Queensland Press, St Lucia, 1975, p. 199.
8 Hunt, *This Side of Heaven*, p. 291.
9 Glen Withers, 'The 1916–1917 Conscription Referenda: A Cliometric Re-appraisal', *Historical Studies*, 20, 1982, p. 45.
10 McKernan, *Australian Churches at War*, p. 116.
11 McKernan, *Australian Churches at War*, p. 116.
12 Hunt, *This Side of Heaven*, p. 289.
13 First AIF data base.
14 T. P. Boland, *James Duhig*, University of Queensland Press, St Lucia, 1986, p. 263.
15 R. P. Davis, 'Tasmania' in D. J. Murphy (ed.), *Labor in Politics: The State Labor Parties in Australia 1880–1920*, University of Queensland Press, St Lucia, 1975, p. 434.
16 Bede Nairn, *The Big Fella: Jack Lang and the Australian Labor Party 1891–1949*, Melbourne University Press, Melbourne, 1986, p. 28.
17 Nairn, *The Big Fella*, p. 174.
18 Nairn, *The Big Fella*, p. 80.
19 Joan Rydon, *A Federal Legislature: The Australian Commonwealth Parliament 1901–1980*, Oxford University Press, Melbourne, 1980, pp. 140–1.
20 *Census of the Commonwealth of Australia*, 30 June, 1933, pp. 153–5.
21 Campion, *Australian Catholics*, p. 87.
22 L.L. Robson (ed.), *Australian Commentaries: Select Articles from the Round Table 1911–1942*, Melbourne University Press, Melbourne, 1975 p. 135.
23 John McCarthy, 'All For Australia': Some Right Wing Responses to the depression in New South Wales, 1929–1932', *Journal of the Royal Australian Historical Society*, 57, 1971, p. 163.
24 Paul Nicholls, 'Australian Protestantism and the Politics of the Great Depression, 1929–31', *Journal of Religious History*, vol. 17, 1992, p. 212.
25 David Hilliard, *Godliness and Good Order: A History of the Anglican Church of South Australia*, Wakefield Press, Adelaide, 1986, p. 108.
26 Nicholls, 'Australian Protestantism', p. 216.
27 Nicholls, 'Australian Protestantism', p. 215.
28 Peter Hempenstall, *The Meddlesome Priest: A Life of Ernest Burgmann*, Allen &

Unwin, Sydney, 1993, p. 138.

29 Pip Nicholson, 'Merton Hall Women and Professional Life: 1917–38' in Rosslyn McCarthy and Marjorie R. Theobald (eds), *Melbourne Church of England Girls Grammar School: Centenary Essays 1893–1993*, Hyland House, Melbourne, 1993, p. 85.

30 Janet McCalman, *Journeyings: The Biography of a Middle-Class Generation 1920–1990*, Melbourne University Press, Melbourne, 1993, pp. 327–8.

31 Hogan, *The Sectarian Strand*, p. 219.

32 McCalman, *Journeyings*, p. 155.

33 *Census*, 1933, p. 155.

34 D. Wetherell and C. Carr-Gregg, *Camilla: C.H. Wedgwood. A Life*, Sydney, 1990, p. 112.

35 Harris, *One Blood*, p. 556.

36 James Miller, *Koori: A Will to Win: The Heroic Resistance, Survival and Triumph of Black Australia*, Angus & Robertson, Sydney, 1985, p. 128.

37 Janet Mathews, *The Two Worlds of Jimmy Barker*, revised edition, Aboriginal Studies Press, Canberra, 1988, pp. 56, 67.

38 Harris, *One Blood*, p. 591.

39 Harris, *One Blood*, p. 593.

40 Tigger Wise, *The Self-Made Anthropologist: A Life of A.P. Elkin*, Allen & Unwin, Sydney, 1985, p. 66.

41 Wise, *Self-Made Anthropologist*, p. 144.

42 Andrew Markus, *Governing Savages*, Allen & Unwin, Sydney, 1990, pp. 59, 60.

43 Harris, *One Blood*, p. 518.

44 Report of Conference Regarding Payment of Aboriginals and Half-Castes, 1930, p. 55, A1, 38/329, Australian Archives, Canberra.

45 *Official Year Book of the Commonwealth of Australia*, 1942–43, p. 315.

46 *Sydney Morning Herald*, 3 September 1928.

47 McCalman, *Journeyings*, p. 10.

48 Vamplew, *Historical Statistics*, pp. 26, 428-35. The 1936 figure lacks precision because national censuses were only conducted in 1933 and 1947.

5. Preservation of Christian Australia

1 Michael McKernan, *All In! Australia During the Second World War*, Thomas Nelson, Melbourne, 1983, pp. 3, 5.

2 Hempenstall, *The Meddlesome Priest*, p. 212.

3 Frank Engel, *Christians in Australia, Times of Change 1918–1978*, vol. 2, Joint Board of Christian Education, Melbourne, 1993, p. 342.

4 Michael Gilchrist, *Daniel Mannix: Priest & Patriot*, Dove Communications, Melbourne, 1982, p. 177.

5 Boland, *James Duhig*, p. 312.

6 Gilchrist, *Daniel Mannix*, p. 182.

7. McKernan, *All In!*, pp. 255–7.

8 Vamplew, *Historical Statistics*, pp. 26, 421–7, 438.

9 *Census*, 1933, p. 155.

10 Michael Cigler, *The Afghans in Australia*, AE Press, Melbourne, 1986, p. 132.

11 David Hilliard, 'Popular Religion in Australia in the 1950s: A study of Adelaide and Brisbane', *Journal of Religious History*, vol. 15, 1989, p. 219.
12 McCalman, *Journeyings*, p. 236.
13 Hilliard, 'Popular Religion', p. 219.
14 Vamplew, *Historical Statistics*, p. 438; Robert Currie, Alan Gilbert and Lee Horsley, *Churches and Churchgoers: Patterns of Church Growth in the British Isles since 1700*, Clarendon Press, Oxford, 1977, p. 187.
15 See Edmund Campion, *Rockhoppers: Growing up Catholic in Australia*, Penguin, Ringwood, 1982.
16 Hogan, *Sectarian Strand*, p. 2.
17 Judith Brett, *Robert Menzies' Forgotten People*, Pan Macmillan, Sydney, 1992, p. 62.
18 John Warhurst, 'Catholics, Communism and the Australian Party System', *Politics*, 14, 1979, p. 231.
19 Gerard Henderson, *Mr. Santamaria and the Bishops*, St Patrick's College, Sydney, 1982, p. 28.
20 Paul Ormonde, *The Movement*, Thomas Nelson, Sydney, 1972, p. 35.
21 Mark Bray and Malcolm Rimmer, *Delivering the Goods: A History of the NSW Transport Workers Union 1888–1986*, Allen & Unwin, Sydney, 1987, p. 174.
22 Graham Freudenberg, *Cause for Power: the Official History of the New South Wales Branch of the Labor Party*, Pluto Press, Sydney, 1991, p. 224.
23 Vamplew, pp. 26, 421–22; D. W. Rawson, *Australia Votes: The 1958 Federal Election*, Melbourne University Press, Melbourne, 1961, pp. 211–43.
24 R. N. Spann, 'The Catholic Vote in Australia' in Henry Mayer (ed.), *Catholics and the Free Society: An Australian Symposium*, Cheshire, Melbourne, 1961, p. 116.
25 Robert A. Hall, *The Black Diggers: Aborigines and Torres Strait Islanders in the Second World War*, Allen & Unwin, Sydney, 1989, p. 170.
26 Hall, *The Black Diggers*, p. 176.
27 Wright and Clancy, *The Methodists*, p. 194.

6. The making of Post-Christian Australia

1 Hans Mol, *Religion in Australia: A Sociological Investigation*, Sydney, 1971, pp. 15–16.
2 Mol, *Religion in Australia*, chs. 5, 12; Hans Mol, *The Faith of Australians*, Thomas Nelson, Sydney, 1985, p. 176.
3 Gary D. Bouma and Beverley R. Dixon, *The Religious Factor in Australian Life*, MARC Australia, Melbourne, 1986.
4 Ken Dempsey, 'Inequality, Belonging and Religion in a Rural Community' in Alan W. Black (ed.), *Religion in Australia: Sociological Perspectives*, Sydney, 1991, p. 69.
5 Hugh Stretton, *Political Essays*, Georgian House, Melbourne, 1987, ch. 14.
6 David Hilliard and Arnold Hunt, 'Religion' in Richards (ed.), p. 224.
7 M. A. Jones, *The Australian Welfare State: Origins, Control and Choices*, 3rd edition, Allen & Unwin, Sydney, 1990, pp. 45–8.

8 Freudenberg, *Cause for Power*, p. 239.
9 Greg Langley, *A Decade of Dissent: Vietnam and the Conflict on the Homefront*, Allen & Unwin, Sydney, 1992, p. 12.
10 Vamplew, *Historical Statistics*, pp. 444–5. Mol, *Religion in Australia*, p. 291.
11 D. A. Kemp, *Society and Electoral Behaviour in Australia: A Study of Three Decades*, University of Queensland Press, St Lucia, 1978, ch. 6; Bouma and Dixon, *The Religious Factor*, pp. 31–2.
12 Kenneth Dempsey, *Conflict and Decline: Ministers and Laymen in an Australian Country Town*, Methuen, Sydney, 1983, p. 53.
13 Norman W. H. Blaikie, *The Plight of the Australian Clergy: To Convert, Care or Challenge?* University of Queensland Press, St Lucia, 1979, pp. 79–82, 156, 231.
14 John Spooner, *The Golden See. Diocese of Ballarat: The Anglican Church in Western Victoria*, J. Ferguson Ltd., Sydney, 1989, pp. 239–40.
15 Campion, *Rockhoppers*, p. 172.
16 Catholic Commission for Justice and Peace, *Justice Trends*, no. 18, 1981.
17 Personal discussion.
18 Gillian Cowlishaw, *Black, White or Brindle: Race in Rural Australia*, Cambridge University Press, Cambridge, 1988, pp. 115–7.
19 Harris, *One Blood*, p. 811.
20 Robert Stringer, 'The Western Australian Churches' Response to Aboriginal Land Rights, 1970–1985' in John Tonkin (ed.), *Religion and Society in Western Australia*, University of Western Australia Press, Nedlands, 1987, p. 165.
21 Grace Koch (ed.), *Katetye Country: An Aboriginal History of the Barrow Creek Area*, Institute for Aboriginal Development Publications, Alice Springs, 1993, p. 131.
22 Grace Koch, 'Syncretic Sacred Music (Gospel, Jesus Purlapa)', unpublished MS, 1993.
23 Martin Flanagan, 'Fighting to Bridge the Gap', *Age*, 15 August 1992.
24 Anne O'Brien, '"A Church Full of Men". Masculinism and the Church in Australian History', *Australian Historical Studies*, 25, 1993, pp. 437–57.
25 Elizabeth Wood Ellem (ed.), *The Church Made Whole: National Conference on Women in the Uniting Church 1990*, David Lovell Publishing, Melbourne, 1990, p. 13.
26 Australian Bureau of Statistics, *1991 Census of Population and Housing: State Comparison Series: Religion*, Canberra, 1993.
27 Bureau of Migration Research, *Birthplace, Language, Religion 1971–86*, Canberra, 1991, vol. 3, p. 127.
28 Gary Bouma, 'Religious Identification in Australia: 1981 to 1991', *People and Place*, 1, 1993, pp. 13–17.
29 *Age*, 28 August 1993.
30 Ian McAllister, *Political Behaviour: Citizens, Parties and Elites in Australia*, Longman, Melbourne, 1992, pp. 141–2.

Bibliography

Age, Melbourne.

ATA, ABE (1) Wade (ed.), *Religion and Ethnic Identity: An Australian Study*, 3 vols, Spectrum Publications, Burwood, 1988–90.

Atkinson, Alan and Aveling, Marian, (eds), *Australians 1838*, Fairfax, Syme & Weldon, Sydney, 1987.

Austin, A.G., *Australian Education 1788–1900: Church, State and Public Education in Colonial Australia*, Pitman, Melbourne, 1961.

Australian Bureau of Statistics, *1991 Census of Population and Housing*, Canberra, 1993.

Australian Dictionary of Biography, vols 1–13, Melbourne University Press, Abacada Press, Melbourne, 1966–1993.

Badger, C.R., *The Reverend Charles Strong and the Australian Church*, Abacada Press, Melbourne, 1971.

Baker, D.W.A., *Days of Wrath: A Life of John Dunmore Lang*, Melbourne University Press, Melbourne, 1985.

Bannister, Robert C., *Social Darwinism: Science and Myth in Anglo-American Social Thought*, Temple University Press, Philadelphia, 1979.

Barrett, John, *That Better Country: The Religious Aspect of Life in Eastern Australia, 1835–1850*, Melbourne University Press, Melbourne, 1966.

Black, Alan W. (ed.), *Religion in Australia: Sociological Perspectives*, Allen & Unwin, Sydney, 1991.

Blaikie, Norman W.H., *The Plight of the Australian Clergy: To Convert, Care or Challenge?*, University of Queensland Press, St Lucia, 1979.

Body, A.H., *Firm Still You Stand: The Anglican Church of St John the Baptist Canberra, its Parish and Parishioners 1841–1984*, St Johns Parish Council, Canberra, 1986.

Boland, T.P., *James Duhig*, University of Queensland Press, St Lucia, 1986.

Bollen, J.D., *Protestantism and Social Reform in New South Wales 1890–1910*, Melbourne University Press, Melbourne, 1972.

Boucé, Paul-Gabriel (ed.), *Sexuality in Eighteenth Century Britain*, Manchester University Press, Manchester, 1982.

Bouma, Gary D. and Dixon, Beverley R., *The Religious Factor in Australian Life*, MARC Australia, Melbourne, 1986.

Bouma, Gary, 'Religious Identification in Australia: 1981 to 1991', *People and Place*, vol. 1, 1993.
Bouquet, A.C., *Comparative Religion: A Short Outline*, Penguin, Harmondsworth, 1969.
Bradley, Ian, *The Call to Seriousness: The Evangelical Impact on the Victorians*, Cape, London, 1976.
Bray, Mark and Rimmer, Malcolm, *Delivering the Goods: A History of the NSW Transport Workers Union 1888–1986*, Allen & Unwin, Sydney, 1987.
Brett, Judith, *Robert Menzies' Forgotten People*, Pan Macmillan, Sydney, 1992.
Breward, Ian, *A History of the Australian Churches*, Allen & Unwin, Sydney, 1993.
Broome, Richard, *Treasure in Earthen Vessels: Protestant Christianity in New South Wales Society 1900–1914*, University of Queensland Press, St Lucia, 1980.
Bureau of Migration Research, *Birthplace. Language, Religion 1971–86*, Australian Government Publishing Service, Canberra, 1991.
Burgmann, Verity, *'In Our Time': Socialism and the Rise of Labour, 1885–1905*, Allen & Unwin, Sydney, 1985.
Bygott, Ursula M., *With Pen and Tongue: The Jesuits in Australia 1865–1939*, Melbourne University Press, Melbourne, 1980.
Byrne, Neil J., *Robert Dunne: Archbishop of Brisbane*, University of Queensland Press, St Lucia, 1991.
Cahill, A.E., 'Catholics and Socialism: The 1905 Controversy in Australia', *Journal of Religious History*, vol. 1, 1960.
Cameron, Clyde, *The Confessions of Clyde Cameron*, ABC Enterprises, Sydney, 1990.
Campion, Edmund, *Rockhoppers: Growing up Catholic in Australia*, Penguin, Ringwood, 1982.
Campion, Edmund, *Australian Catholics*, Penguin, Ringwood, 1987.
Cannon, Michael, *The Land Boomers,* Melbourne University Press, Melbourne, 1966.
Catholic Commission for Justice and Peace, *Justice Trends*, No. 18, 1981.
Census of the Commonwealth of Australia, 30 June, 1933.
Christie, M.F., *Aborigines in Colonial Victoria 1835–86*, Sydney University Press, Sydney, 1979.
Cigler, Michael, *The Afghans in Australia*, AE Press, Melbourne, 1986.
Commonwealth of Australia, Official Year Book, 1942–43.
Cowan, James C., *The Elements of the Aborigine Tradition*, Jacaranda Wiley, Longmead, 1992.
Cowlishaw, Gillian, *Black, White or Brindle: Race in Rural Australia*, Cambridge University Press, Cambridge, 1988.
Crawford, R.M., *'A Bit of a Rebel': The Life and Work of George Arnold Wood*, Sydney University Press, Sydney, 1975.
Critchett, Jan, *A 'Distant Field of Murder': Western District Frontiers 1834–1848*, Melbourne University Press, Melbourne, 1990.
Currie, Robert, Gilbert, Alan and Horsley, Lee, *Churches and Churchgoers: Patterns of Church Growth in the British Isles since 1700*, Clarendon Press, Oxford, 1977.

Davis, R.P., 'Christian Socialism in Tasmania 1890–1920', *Journal of Religious History*, vol. 7, 1972.

Davison, Graeme, Dunston, David and McConville, Chris (eds), *The Outcasts of Melbourne: Essays in Social History*, Allen & Unwin, Sydney, 1985.

Deakin, Alfred, *Federated Australia: Selections from Letters to the Morning Post 1900–1910*, Melbourne University Press, Melbourne, 1968.

Dempsey, Kenneth, *Conflict and Decline: Ministers and Laymen in an Australian Country Town*, Methuen, Melbourne, 1983.

Dingle, A.E., 'The Truly Magnificent Thirst: An Historical Survey of Australian Drinking Habits', *Historical Studies*, vol. 19, 1980.

Dixon, Robert, *The Course of Empire: Neo-Classical Culture in New South Wales 1788–1860*, Oxford University Press, Melbourne, 1986.

Easson, Michael (ed.), *McKell: The Achievements of Sir William McKell,* Allen & Unwin, Sydney, 1988.

Ellis, Julie-Ann, '"Cross-Firing Over the Gulf." The Rift Between Methodism and the Labour Movement in South Australia in the 1890s', *Labour History*, No. 64, 1993.

Ely, Richard, *Unto God and Caesar: Religious Issues in the Emerging Commonwealth, 1891–1906*, Melbourne University Press, Melbourne, 1976.

Ely, Richard, 'The Forgotten Nationalism: Australian Civic Protestantism in the Second World War', *Journal of Australian Studies*, No. 20, 1987.

Engel, Frank, *Christians in Australia*, vol. 2, *Times of Change 1918–1978,* Joint Board of Christian Education, Melbourne, 1993.

Field, L.M., *The Forgotten War: Australian Involvement in the South African Conflict of 1899–1902*, Melbourne University Press, Melbourne, 1966.

First AIF Data Base, Department of History, University College, Australian Defence Force Academy, Canberra.

Fitzgerald, Shirley, *Rising Damp: Sydney 1870–90*, Oxford University Press, Melbourne, 1987.

Fitzgerald, Ross, *From the Dreaming to 1915: A History of Queensland,* University of Queensland Press, St Lucia, 1982.

Fitzgerald, Ross, *From 1915 to the Early 1980s: A History of Queensland*, University of Queensland Press, St Lucia, 1984.

Fitzgerald, Ross and Thornton, Harold, *Labor in Queensland: From the 1880s to 1988*, University of Queensland Press, St Lucia, 1989.

Ford, Patrick, *Cardinal Moran and the A.L.P.*, Melbourne University Press, Melbourne, 1966.

Freudenberg, Graham, *Cause for Power: The Official History of the New South Wales Branch of the Labor Party*, Pluto Press, Sydney, 1991.

Garton, Stephen, *Out of Luck: Poor Australians and Social Welfare 1788–1988*, Allen & Unwin, Sydney, 1990.

Gilbert, Alan D., 'The Conscription Referenda, 1916–17: The Impact of the Irish Crisis', *Historical Studies*, vol. 14, 1969.

Gilbert, Alan D., *Religion and Society in Industrial England: Church, Chapel and Social Change 1740–1914*, Longman, London, 1976.

Gilbert, Alan D., *The Making of Post-Christian Britain: A History of the Secularization of Modern Society*, Longman, London, 1980.

Gilchrist, Michael, *Daniel Mannix: Priest & Patriot*, Dove Communications, Melbourne, 1982.

Green, David and Cromwell, Lawrence, *Mutual Welfare or Welfare State: Australia's Friendly Societies*, Allen & Unwin, Sydney, 1984.

Gregory, J.S., *Church and State: Changing Government Policies towards Religion in Australia; with Particular reference to Victoria since Separation*, Melbourne, 1973.

Gregory, Jenny (ed.), *Western Australia Between the Wars 1919–1939*, University of Western Australia Press, Nedlands, 1990.

Grey, Jeffrey, *A Military History of Australia*, Cambridge University Press, Cambridge, 1990.

Gribble, Ernest, *Forty Years with the Aborigines*, Angus & Robertson, Sydney, 1930.

Gribble, J.B., *Dark Deeds in a Sunny Land or Blacks and Whites in North-West Australia*, revised ed., University of Western Australia Press, Nedlands, 1987.

Grimshaw, Patricia, McConville, Chris and McEwan, Ellen (eds), *Families in Colonial Australia*, Allen & Unwin, Sydney, 1985.

Grocott, Allan M., *Convicts, Clergymen and Churches: Attitudes of Convicts and Ex-Convicts towards the Churches and Clergy in NewSouth Wales from 1788 to 1851*, Sydney University Press, Sydney, 1980.

Hall, Robert A., *The Black Diggers: Aborigines and Torres Strait Islanders in the Second World War*, Allen & Unwin, Sydney, 1989.

Hamilton, Celia, 'Irish Catholics of New South Wales and the Labor Party, 1890–1910', *Historical Studies: Australia and New Zealand*, vol. 8, 1958.

Harmstorf, Ian and Cigler, Michael, *The Germans in Australia*, AE Press, Melbourne, 1985.

Harris, John, *One Blood. 200 Years of Aboriginal Encounter with Christianity: A Story of Hope*, Albatross Books, Sutherland, 1990.

Hart, Max, *A Story of Fire: Aboriginal Christianity*, New Creation Publications, Blackwood, 1988.

Hatcher, William S. and Martin, J. Douglas, *The Bah'ai Faith: The Emerging Global Religion*, Harper & Row, San Francisco, 1985.

Hearn, Mark, *Working Lives: A History of the Australian Railways Union (NSW Branch)*, Hale & Iremonger, Sydney, 1990.

Hempenstall, Peter, *The Meddlesome Priest: A Life of Ernest Burgmann*, Allen & Unwin, Sydney, 1993.

Henderson, Gerard, *Mr. Santamaria and the Bishops*, St Patrick's College, Sydney, 1982.

Hicks, Neville T., *This Sin and Scandal: Australia's Population Debate 1891–1911*, Australian National University Press, Canberra, 1978.

Hilliard, David, *Godliness and Good Order: A History of the Anglican Church of South Australia*, Wakefield Press, Adelaide, 1986.

Hilliard, David, 'Popular Religion in Australia in the 1950s: A study of Adelaide and Brisbane', *Journal of Religious History*, vol. 15, 1989.

Hogan, Michael C., *The Catholic Campaign for State Aid*, Catholic Theological Faculty, Sydney, 1978.

Hogan, Michael C., *The Sectarian Strand: Religion in Australian History*, Penguin, Ringwood, 1987.

Howe, Renate, 'Christian Socialism and the Emergence of Public Housing', *St Mark's Review*, No. 153, 1993.

Hudson, W.J., *Casey*, Oxford University Press, Melbourne, 1986.

Hunt, Arnold D., *This Side of Heaven: A History of Methodism in South Australia*, Lutheran Publishing House, Adelaide, 1985

Hyam, Ronald, *Empire and Sexuality: The British Experience*, Manchester University Press, Manchester, 1990.

Jackson, H.R., *Churches and People in Australia and New Zealand 1860–1930*, Allen & Unwin, Wellington, 1987.

Johnson, Audrey, *Fly a Rebel Flag: Bill Morrow 1888–1980*, Penguin, Ringwood, 1986.

Jones, M.A., *The Australian Welfare State: Origins, Control and Choices*, 3rd edition, Allen & Unwin, Sydney, 1990.

Judd, Stephen & Cable, Kenneth, *Sydney Anglicans: A History of the Dioceses*, Anglican Information Office, Sydney, 1987.

Kaldor, Peter, *Who Goes Where? Who Doesn't Care*, Lancer Books, Sydney, 1987.

Kaldor, Peter, et. al., *First Look in the Mirror: Initial Findings of the 1991 National Church Life Survey*, ANZEA Publishers, Sydney, 1992.

Kemp, D.A., *Society and Electoral Behaviour in Australia: A Study of Three Decades*, University of Queensland Press, St Lucia, 1978.

Kennedy, Brian, *Silver, Sin and Sixpenny Ale: A Social History of Broken Hill 1883–1921*, Melbourne University Press, Melbourne, 1978.

Kiddle, Margaret, *Caroline Chisolm*, Melbourne University Press, Melbourne, 1950.

Kirkby, Diane, *Alice Henry: The Power of Pen and Voice. The Life of an Australian-American Labor Reformer*, Cambridge University Press, Cambridge, 1991.

Koch, Grace (ed.), *Katetye Country: An Aboriginal History of the Barrow Creek Area*, Institute of Aboriginal Development Publications, Alice Springs, 1993.

Koch, Grace, 'Syncretic Sacred Music (Gospel, Jesus Purlapa)', unpublished MS, 1993.

Lake, Marilyn, *A Divided Society: Tasmania During World War I*, Melbourne University Press, Melbourne, 1975.

Langley, Greg, *A Decade of Dissent: Vietnam and the Conflict on the Homefront*, Allen & Unwin, Sydney, 1992.

Langmore, Diane, *Prime Ministers' Wives: The Public and Private Lives of Ten Australian Women*, McPhee Gribble, Melbourne, 1992.

Lawson, Ronald, *Brisbane in the 1890s: A Study of an Australian Urban Society*, University of Queensland Press, St Lucia, 1973.

Lees, Stella and Senyard, June, *The 1950s... How Australia became a Modern Society, and Everyone got a House and a Car*, Hyland House, Melbourne, 1987.

Loos, Noel, 'The Australian Board of Missions, the Anglican Church and the Aborigines 1850–1900', *Journal of Religious History*, vol. 17, 1992.

Loos, Noel and Keast, Robyn, 'The Radical Promise: The Aboriginal Christian Cooperative Movement', *Australian Historical Studies*, vol. 25, 1992.

McAllister, Ian, *Political Behaviour: Citizens, Parties and Elites in Australia*, Longman, Melbourne, 1992.

McCalman, Janet, *Struggletown: Public and Private Life in Richmond 1900–1965*, Melbourne University Press, Melbourne, 1984.

McCalman, Janet, *Journeyings: The Biography of a Middle-Class Generation 1920–1990*, Melbourne University Press, Melbourne, 1993.

McCarthy, John, 'All For Australia': Some Right Wing Responses to the Depression in New South Wales, 1929–1932', *Journal of the Royal Australian Historical Society*, vol. 57, 1971.

McCarthy, Rosslyn and Theobald, Marjorie R. (eds), *Melbourne Church of England Girls Grammar School: Centenary Essays 1893–1993*, Hyland House, Melbourne, 1993.

McConville, Chris and McEwen, Ellen (eds), *Families in Colonial Australia*, Allen & Unwin, Sydney, 1985.

McGrath, Ann, '*Born to Cattle*': *Aborigines in Cattle Country*, Allen & Unwin, Sydney, 1987.

Macintosh, Neil K, *Richard Johnson: Chaplain to the Colony of New South Wales. His Life and Times 1755–1827*, Pilgrim International, Sydney, 1978.

McKernan, Michael, *Australian Churches at War: Attitudes and Activities of the Major Churches, 1914–1918*, Southwood Press, Sydney, 1980.

McKernan, Michael, *All In! Australia During the Second World War*, Thomas Nelson, Melbourne, 1983.

McLeod, Hugh, *Religion and the Working Class in Nineteenth-Century Britain*, Macmillan, London, 1984.

McMullin, Ross, *The Light on the Hill: The Australian Labor Party, 1891–1991*, Oxford University Press, Melbourne, 1991.

Mansfield, John, 'The Christian Social Order Movement 1943–51', *Journal of Religious History*, vol. 15, 1988.

Mansfield, John, 'The Social Gospel and the Church of England in New South Wales in the 1930s', *Journal of Religious History*, vol. 13, 1985.

Markus, Andrew, *Blood from a Stone: William Cooper and the Australian Aborigines League*, Allen & Unwin, Sydney, 1988.

Markus, Andrew, *Governing Savages*, Allen & Unwin, Sydney, 1990.

Martin, A.W., 'Henry Parkes and the Political Manipulation of Sectarianism', *Journal of Religious History*, vol. 9, 1976.

Martin, A.W., *Henry Parkes: A Biography*, Melbourne University Press, Melbourne, 1980.

Martin, A.W., *Robert Menzies: A Life*, vol.1, Melbourne University Press, Melbourne, 1993.

Mathews, Janet, *The Two Worlds of Jimmy Barker*, revised edition, Aboriginal Studies Press, Canberra, 1988.

Mayne, A.J.C., *Fever, Squalor and Vice: Sanitation and Social Policy in Victorian Sydney*, University of Queensland Press, St Lucia, 1982.

Miller, James, *Koori: A Will to Win: The Heroic Resistance, Survival and Triumph of Black Australia*, Angus & Robertson, Sydney, 1985.

Mol, Hans, *Religion in Australia: A Sociological Investigation*, Nelson, Sydney, 1971.

Mol, Hans, *The Faith of Australians*, Allen & Unwin, Sydney, 1985.

Moses, John A.,'Canon David John Garland and the ANZAC Tradition', *St Mark's Review*, No. 54, 1993.

Moss, Jim, *The Sound of Trumpets: History of the Labour Movement in South Australia*, Wakefield Press, Netley, 1985.
Mukherjee, S. K., Walker J. R., and Jacobsen, E. N., *Crime and Punishment in the Colonies: A Statistical Profile*, History Project Inc., Kensington, 1988.
Mulder, John M. and Wilson, John F. (eds), *Religion in American History: Interpretive Essays*, Prentice Hall, Englewood Cliffs, 1978.
Mulvaney, D.J. and White, Peter J. (eds), *Australians to 1788*, Fairfax, Syme & Weldon, Sydney, 1987.
Murphy, D.J., Joyce, R.B. & Hughes, Colin A. (eds), *Prelude to Power: The Rise of the Labour Party in Queensland*, Milton, 1970.
Murphy, D.J., *T.J. Ryan: A Political Biography*, University of Queensland Press, St Lucia, 1975.
Murphy, D.J. (ed.), *Labor in Politics: The State Labor Parties in Australia 1880–1920*, University of Queensland Press, St Lucia, 1975.
Murphy, D.J. and Joyce, R.B. (eds), *Queensland Political Portraits 1859–1952*, University of Queensland Press, St Lucia, 1978.
Murray, Robert, *The Split: Australian Labor in the Fifties*, Cheshire, Melbourne, 1970.
Murray, Robert, and White, Kate, *The Ironworkers: A History of the Federated Ironworkers Association of Australia*, Hale & Iremonger, Sydney, 1982.
Nairn, Bede, *The Big Fella: Jack Lang and the Australian Labor Party 1891–1949*, Melbourne University Press, Melbourne, 1986.
Nicholas, Stephen (ed.), *Convict Workers: Reinterpreting Australia's Past*, Cambridge University Press, Cambridge, 1988.
Nicholls, Paul, 'Australian Protestantism and the Politics of the Great Depression, 1929–31', *Journal of Religious History*, vol. 17, 1992.
Norman, Edward, *The Victorian Christian Socialists*, Cambridge University Press, Cambridge, 1987.
O'Brien, Anne, *Poverty's Prison: the Poor in New South Wales 1880–1918*, Melbourne University Press, Melbourne, 1988.
O'Brien, Anne, '"A Church Full of Men": Masculinism and the Church in Australian History', *Australian Historical Studies*, vol. 25, 1993.
O'Brien, J.M., 'Sectarianism in the New South Wales Elections of 1843 and 1856', *Journal of Religious History*, vol. 9, 1976.
O'Farrell, P. J., 'The History of the New South Wales Labour Movement, 1880–1914: A Religious Interpretation', *Journal of Religious History*, vol. 2, 1962.
O'Farrell, P. J., *Harry Holland: Militant Socialist*, Australian National University Press, Canberra, 1964.
O'Farrell, Patrick, *The Catholic Church and Community in Australia: A History*, Thomas Nelson, Sydney, 1977.
Official Year Book of the Commonwealth of Australia, 1942–43.
Oldfield, Audrey, *Woman Suffrage in Australia: A Gift or a Struggle?*, Cambridge University Press, Cambridge, 1992.
Ormonde, Paul, *The Movement*, Thomas Nelson, Sydney, 1972.
Parkin, Andrew and Patience, Allen (eds), *The Dunstan Decade: Social Democracy at the State Level*, Longman, Melbourne, 1981.

Pattel-Gray, Anne, *Through Aboriginal Eyes: The Cry from the Wilderness*, WCC Publications, Geneva, 1991.

Pawsey, Margaret M., *The Popish Plot: Culture Clashes in Victoria 1860–1863*, St. Patrick's College, Sydney, 1983.

Phillips, Walter, 'Religious Profession and Practice in N.S.W., 1850–1901: The Statistical Evidence, *Historical Studies*, vol. 15, No. 59, 1972.

Phillips, Walter, *Defending 'A Christian Century': Churchmen and Society in New South Wales in the 1880s and After*, University of Queensland Press, St Lucia, 1981.

Piggin, Stuart, *Faith of Steel: A History of the Christian Churches in Illawarra, Australia*, University of Wollongong, Wollongong, 1984.

Pike, Douglas, *Paradise of Dissent: South Australia 1829–1857*, Cambridge University Press, London, 1957.

Porter, Robert, *Paul Hasluck: A Political Biography*, University of Western Australia Press, Perth, 1993.

Powell, Alan, *Patrician Democrat: The Political Life of Charles Cowper 1843–1870*, Melbourne University Press, Melbourne, 1977.

Quaife, G.R., 'Religion and Colonial Politics: State Aid and Sectarianism in Victoria, 1856', *Journal of Religious History*, vol. 10, 1978.

Radi, Heather, Spearitt, Peter and Hinton, Elizabeth, *Biographical Register of the New South Wales Parliament 1901–1970*, Australian National University Press, Canberra, 1979.

Rae-Ellis, Vivienne, *Black Robinson: Protector of Aborigines*, Melbourne University Press, Melbourne, 1988.

Raftery, Judith, 'Betting Shops, Soup Kitchens and Well-Kept Sundays: The Response of the South Australian Churches to Some Social Issues, 1919–39', *Journal of Religious History*, vol. 16, 1991.

Rawson, D.W., *Australia Votes: The 1958 Federal Election*, Melbourne University Press, Melbourne, 1961.

Reece, Bob and Stannage, Tom (eds), *European–Aboriginal Relations in Western Australian History*, University of Western Australia, Perth, 1984.

Reed, Rosslyn, 'Calvinism, the Weber Thesis, and Entrepreneurial Behaviour: the Case of David Syme', *Journal of Religious History*, vol. 16, 1991.

Reid, Gordon, *A Picnic with the Natives: Aboriginal–European Relations in the Northern Territory to 1990*, Melbourne University Press, Melbourne, 1990.

Report of Conference Regarding Payment of Aboriginals and Half-Castes, 1930, A1, 38/329, Australian Archives, Canberra.

Reynolds, Henry, *Aborigines and Settlers*, Cassell, Melbourne, 1972.

Reynolds, P.L., *The Democratic Labor Party*, Jacaranda, Milton, 1974.

Richards, Eric (ed.), *The Flinders History of South Australia: Social History*, Wakefield Press, Adelaide, 1986.

Rickard, John, *Class and Politics: New South Wales, Victoria and the Early Commonwealth*, Australia National University Press, Canberra, 1976.

Ritchie, John, *Lachlan Macquarie: A Biography*, Melbourne University Press, Melbourne, 1986.

Robin, A. de Q., *Charles Perry Bishop of Melbourne: The Challenges of a Colonial Episcopate, 1847–76*, University of Western Australia Press, Nedlands, 1968.

Robinson, Portia, *The Women of Botany Bay*, Macquarie Library, Sydney, 1988.
Robson, L.L. (ed.), *Australian Commentaries: Select Articles from the Round Table 1911–1942*, Melbourne University Press, Melbourne, 1975.
Robson, Lloyd, *A History of Tasmania*, 2 vols, Oxford University Press, Melbourne, 1983, 1991.
Roe, Michael, *Quest for Authority in Eastern Australia 1835–1851*, Melbourne University Press, Melbourne, 1965.
Ross, Edgar, *A History of the Miners' Federation of Australia*, Australasian Coal and Shale Employees' Federation, Sydney, 1970.
Rubinstein, Hilary L, *Chosen: The Jews in Australia*, Heinemann, Sydney, 1987.
Rubinstein, W. D. (ed.), *Jews in the Sixth Continent*, Allen & Unwin, Sydney, 1987.
Rubinstein, W. D. *The Jews in Australia*, Heinemann, Blackburn, 1986.
Rydon, Joan, *A Biographical Register of the Commonwealth Parliament 1901–1972*, Australian National University Press, Canberra, 1975.
Rydon, Joan, *A Federal Legislature: The Australian Commonwealth Parliament 1901–1980*, Oxford University Press, Melbourne, 1980.
Salvado, Dom Rosendo, *The Salvado Memoirs*, ed. E.J. Stormon, University of Western Australia Press, Nedlands, 1977.
Santamaria, B. A., *Against the Tide*, Oxford University Press, Melbourne, 1981.
Santamaria, B. A., *Daniel Mannix: The Quality of Leadership*, Melbourne University Press, Melbourne, 1984.
Serle, Geoffrey, *The Golden Age: A History of the Colony of Victoria 1851–1861*, Melbourne University Press, Melbourne, 1963.
Serle, Geoffrey, *The Rush to be Rich: A History of the Colony of Victoria*, Melbourne University Press, Melbourne, 1971.
Shaw, G. P., *Patriarch and Patriot: William Grant Broughton 1788–1853*, Melbourne University Press, Melbourne, 1978.
Sheridan, Tom, *Division of Labour: Industrial Relations in the Chifley Years, 1945–49*, Oxford University Press, Melbourne, 1989.
Short, Susana, *Laurie Short: A Political Life*, Allen & Unwin, Sydney, 1992.
Sigwerth, Eric M. (ed.), *In Search of Victorian Values: Aspects of Nineteenth-Century Thought and Society*, Manchester University Press, Manchester, 1988.
Smith, F. B., 'Spiritualism in Victoria in the Nineteenth Century', *Journal of Religious History*, vol. 3, 1965.
Spann, R. N., 'The Catholic vote in Australia' in Mayer, Henry (ed.), *Catholics and the Free Society: An Australian Symposium*, Cheshire, Melbourne, 1961.
Spooner, John, *The Golden See. Diocese of Ballarat: The Anglican Church in Western Victoria*, J. Ferguson Ltd., Sydney, 1989.
Stevens, Christine, *Tin Mosques and Ghantowns: A History of Afghan Cameldrivers in Australia*, Oxford University Press, Melbourne, 1989.
Stretton, Hugh, *Political Essays*, Georgian House, Melbourne, 1987.
Sturma, M., *Vice in a Vicious Society: Crime and Convicts in Mid-Nineteenth Century New South Wales*, University of Queensland Press, St. Lucia, 1983.
Swain, Tony and Rose, Deborah Bird (eds), *Aboriginal Australians and Christian Missions: Ethnographic and Historical Studies*, Australian Association for the Study of Religion, Bedford Park, 1988.

Teale, Ruth (ed.), *Colonial Eve: Sources on Women in Australia 1788–1914*, Oxford University Press, Melbourne, 1978.

Thorpe, William, 'Archibald Meston and Aboriginal Legislation in Colonial Queensland', *Historical Studies*, vol. 21, 1984.

Tonkin, John (ed.), *Religion and Society in Western Australia*, University of Western Australia Press, Nedlands, 1987.

Travers, Robert, *The Phantom Fenians of New South Wales*, Kangaroo Press, Sydney, 1986.

Turner, Ian, *Industrial Labour and Politics: The Dynamics of the Labour Movement in Eastern Australia*, Australian National University Press, Canberra, 1965.

Tyrrell, Ian, 'International Aspects of the Woman's Temperance Movement in Australia: The Influence of the American WCTU, 1882–1914', *Journal of Religious History*, vol. 12, 1983.

Vamplew, Wray (ed.), *Australians: Historical Statistics*, Fairfax, Syme & Weldon, Sydney, 1987.

Wanna, John, 'A Paradigm of Consent: Explanations of Working Class Moderation in South Australia', *Labour History*, No. 52, 1987.

Warhurst, John, 'Catholics, Communism and the Australian Party System', *Politics*, vol. 14, 1979.

Wetherell, D. and Carr-Gregg, C., *Camilla: C.H. Wedgwood. A Life*, University New South Wales Press, Sydney, 1990.

Whip, Rosemary and Hughes, Colin A. (eds), *Political Crossroads: The 1989 Queensland Election*, University of Queensland Press, St Lucia, 1991.

Whitton, Evan, *The Hillbilly Dictator: Australia's Police State*, revised edition, ABC, Sydney, 1993.

Willis, Sabine (ed.), *Women, Faith and Fetes: Essays in the History of Women and the Church in Australia*, Dove Communications, Melbourne, 1977.

Wischer, John (ed.), *The Presbyterians of Toorak*, The Dominion Press, Melbourne, 1975.

Wise, Tigger, *The Self-Made Anthropologist: A Life of A.P. Elkin*, Allen & Unwin, Sydney, 1985.

Withers, Glen, 'The 1916–1917 Conscription Referenda: A Cliometric Re-appraisal', *Historical Studies*, vol. 20, 1982.

Ward, Russell and Robertson, John (eds.), *Such was Life: Select Documents in Australian Social History*, 3 vols, Alternative Publishing Company, Chippendale, 1978–86.

Ward, Russell and Aveling, Marian (eds.), *Australians 1838,* Fairfax, Syme & Weldon, Sydney, 1987.

Wood Ellem, Elizabeth (ed.), *The Church Made Whole: National Conference on Women in the Uniting Church 1990*, David Lovell Publishers, Melbourne, 1990.

Woolmington, Jean (ed.), *Religion in Early Australia: The Problem of Church and State*, Cassell, Sydney, 1976.

Wright, Don and Clancy, Eric, *The Methodists: A History of Methodism in New South Wales*, Allen & Unwin, Sydney, 1993.

Yarwood, A.T., *Samuel Marsden: The Great Survivor*, Melbourne, 1977.

Index